D0471345

Gottfried, Ted.
Alan Turing : the
architect of the computer
c1996.
33305007835626
LA   07/09/97

ALAN TURING

The ARCHITECT of the COMPUTER AGE

BY TED GOTTFRIED

AN IMPACT BIOGRAPHY
FRANKLIN WATTS
A DIVISION OF GROLIER PUBLISHING
NEW YORK   LONDON   HONG KONG   SYDNEY
DANBURY, CONNECTICUT

SANTA CLARA COUNTY LIBRARY

3 3305 00783 5626

*Note to readers: English spellings in quoted material have been
Americanized*

*Photographs ©: Kings College, Cambridge University Library: 1 (both pho-
tos); The Bettmann Archive: 2, 3, 4; American Institute of Physics, Emilio
Segre Visual Archives/Richard Arens: 5; UPI/Bettmann: 6; The Computer
Museum: 7; Times Newspapers Limited: 8 bottom, 8 top (Bill Warhurst);
UPI/Bettmann: 9; The Computer Museum: 10 top; Kings College, Cambridge
University Library: 10 bottom, 11; University of Manchester: 12-13, 13 inset,
14; UPI/Bettmann: 15; NASA: 16.*

Library of Congress Cataloging-in-Publication Data

Gottfried, Ted.
Alan Turing : the architect of the computer age / by Ted Gottfried.
p. cm. — (An Impact biography)
Includes bibliographical references (p. –) and index.
ISBN 0-531-11287-X
1. Turing, Alan Mathison, 1912–1954—Juvenile literature.
2. Mathematicians—Great Britain—Biography—Juvenile literature.
I. Title. II. Series.
QA29.T8G68 1996
510'.92—dc20   96-18797
                                                                  CIP   AC

©1996 by Ted Gottfried
All rights reserved. Published simultaneously in Canada.
Printed in the United States of America.
1 2 3 4 5 6 7 8 9 10 R 05 04 03 02 01 00 99 98 97 96

This one is for Janet Bode, whose commitment to her craft and devotion to her readers continues to set the standard for all of us who write for young adults.
—Peace and Love

ACKNOWLEDGMENTS

Many thanks to Peter Brooks, inventor, teacher, president of Micromind, Inc., and developer of the first low-cost stereoscopic virtual reality system for the IBM PC. His guidance and technical advice were an invaluable contribution to this book. Any shortcomings, however, are mine alone.

I am grateful to the staff of the American Institute of Physics in New York City for their assistance. Thanks also to personnel of various branches of the New York Public Library, as well as to those at the research library who helped me access a rare copy of the Turing memoir written by his mother.

The support of my two editors—E. Russell Primm, III, who has believed in this project from the first, and James Taft, whose cool logic and patience during the editing process directed my attention to technical blunders—is much appreciated. Gratitude is also due my writer buddy Janet Bode, who listened to my kvetching while booting up her next chapter with one hand and eating peanut butter out of the jar with the other. Finally, I want to thank my wife, Harriet Gottfried, who—as always—read and critiqued each chapter of this book as it was written.

CONTENTS

BREAKING THE ENIGMA

One early summer day in 1940 during the first year of Word War II, an English farmer looked up from his fields and saw a disheveled young man riding a bicycle on the road to Shenley. There was a small folded baby carriage mounted on the rear of the bike and a neatly tied package in the basket on the handlebars. Not a cloud in the sky, no enemy planes, and yet the rider was wearing a gas mask. His name was Alan Turing.

He suffered from hay fever and wore the gas mask to screen out pollen generated by the weeds in the fields. The package in the basket contained two ingots of pure silver. Turing had become convinced that a German invasion of England was imminent and that under a Nazi occupation the value of British currency would plummet. He had converted his savings and was now on his way to bury the silver bars.

Before reaching the village of Shenley, Turing parked the bike, loaded the silver into the baby carriage, and wheeled it deep into the woods. He dug a deep hole and buried one of the bars in a grove of trees. He buried the other under a bridge spanning a stream. He recorded the two locations in his own secret code, put the paper in an old Benzedrine inhaler, and hid it under a second bridge. Then he returned to his bicycle. The ride back was filled with pain because Turing had injured his back digging.

Some months later, on the morning of November 11, 1940, halfway around the world on the Indian Ocean, the captain of the British merchant ship *Automedan* was on the bridge when the German raider *Atlantis* fired the first of twenty-eight rounds. He died instantly. The shells that followed killed almost all of the ship's officers and crew.

When the Germans boarded the *Automedan* they found a packet of top-secret documents bound for Singapore. Among them were Admiralty intelligence reports, minutes of the British War Cabinet's meetings (which revealed an inability to defend British holdings and shipping lanes in the Far East against Japan), and copies of the *British Merchant Navy Code*. These documents were delivered to German admiral Paul Wenneker in Tokyo, who judged them to be "of the very greatest significance."[1]

Knowledge of the *Code* helped the Germans sink one fifth (3,500,000 tons) of the British merchant fleet by the end of the war. This would be done largely by Nazi submarines, called *U-boats*. The *British Merchant Navy Code* was encoded by a German coding device called the *Enigma machine*. It was then transmitted by radio to the U-boat commanders. As long as the *Enigma codes* could not be broken, the Germans could organize military operations and adapt to changing circumstances with a speed the world came to know as *blitzkrieg* ("lightning war").

Even before the capture of the *Automedan*, the Nazi U-boats had plagued British shipping convoys. After France surrendered to Germany earlier in 1940, Nazi forces closed off the nearest European ports to British shipping. The only way the British Isles could be supplied with food, clothing, fuel, and armaments was by shipping them from overseas. Its dominions— Canada, Australia, New Zealand, etc.—and the United States were the main providers. U-boats, because they were able to travel underwater, easily preyed on British shipping vessels, making it difficult for Britain to import enough goods to subsist. The capture of the *British Merchant Navy Code*, which gave the Germans advance knowledge of the routes the British merchant ship convoys would take, made the situation even more bleak for Britain. By mid-1941, a half year after the capture of the *Automedan*, Nazi U-boats were sinking 200,000 tons of British shipping a month. Enigma was essential to this high "kill" ratio.

Arthur Scherbius, a German engineer, invented Enigma in the 1920s. It consisted of a typewriter keyboard wired to an electric screen on which any letter of the alphabet could be illuminated. When a letter key was struck, an electric current traveled through an electrically wired rotor to a light bulb on the screen, which would light up a letter. The illuminated letter, however, would not be the same as the letter hit on the keyboard. Striking *B*, for example, might light up *D*. Each time a key was struck, the rotor inside the Enigma device would turn, changing the wirings of the next key stroke for all twenty-six letters. Consequently, striking *B* a second time might light up *P*. The rotor had twenty-six possible initial settings, which corresponded to the letters of the alphabet. Before a message was encoded, the operator of the machine, called the cipher clerk, installed the rotor in any one of the twenty-six initial positions.

Of course, having an Enigma machine was not enough to decode a message. In addition to the machine, the receiver also had to know the initial setting of the rotor. Then, the process could be reversed, and by typing out the gobbledygook letters of an Enigma-encoded message, the original message would light up on the screen. The German military bought Enigma, and during World War II it was their primary encoding device.

The Enigma machines used by the German military were an improvement over the one invented by Scherbius. Instead of the solitary rotor in the original model, the military versions had three rotors that were interchangeable. They could be placed into the machine in any of six combinations, and each rotor could still be set to any of twenty-six positions corresponding to the letters of the alphabet. Multiplying all the possible variations of the initial settings shows that these improvements increased the machine's potential to 105,456 possible connections between keyboard and screen for each keystroke. In addition to the rotors, the military Enigma included additional circuitry, called a plugboard, that raised the possible number of letter conversions to over one billion per keystroke! New initial settings were chosen each day by the cipher clerks. Even if their opponents had a perfect replica of the Enigma machine, they would have to determine the new settings of the machine every day in order to decode German transmissions on a regular basis. The German military was so impressed with their machine that throughout the war they refused to believe that their opponents might be cracking their codes.

Progress on breaking the Enigma code was originally achieved by a Polish team of code breakers in the 1930s. Fearing an invasion by Germany, the Poles had been studying the Enigma machine since 1932, when they received information from the French Secret Service that allowed them to deduce the wirings of the rotors. In addition to building a replica of the Enigma machine, the Poles had devised an ingenious way to determine the initial settings of the rotors and keep up with their daily revisions.

While monitoring German communications, the Poles noticed that a grouping of six letters appeared at the beginning of every message. The specific letters changed for each message, but it always consisted of a six-letter group, such as *EJFOWJ*. The Polish decoders deduced that this must be the code with which the German cipher clerks communicated the initial positions of the rotors to each other. By comparing these six-letter groups to each other while studying a day's transmissions, the Poles were able to determine the settings of the rotors and even unravel the effects of the plugboard. A year of constant monitoring resulted in 105,456 file cards that enabled the decoders to quickly look up the rotor settings based on the six-letter groups.

In September 1938, the German's improved the system with which they communicated initial settings to each other. The Poles were able to devise another method to determine the settings, but it was very time-consuming to do by hand. They built six machines that, using the new method, automatically tested rotor positions until they found the correct settings. These machines were called *Bombes* because they ticked loudly.

The Bombes worked wonderfully for a few months. Then, in December 1938, the Germans increased their stock of rotors from three to six. They would still only use three in the machine at any time, but they could choose them from the larger assortment. This increased the possible arrangements of the rotors from six to sixty. If they were to continue decoding the Enigma messages efficiently, the Polish decoders would have to increase their stock of six Bombes to sixty. They did not have the resources. The Polish decoders invited delegations from France and Britain to Warsaw in July 1939. At the conference, the Poles revealed their secrets to breaking the Enigma code.

Breaking the naval Enigma code had been the number-one priority of British Intelligence since 1938, but until the Warsaw meeting the code had seemed unbreakable. In 1939, British Intelligence set up an elite team of intellectuals in a country mansion called

Bletchley Park. Their job was to pick up where the Polish decoders had left off. Alan Turing, a young mathematician with a "reputation as something of an eccentric," headed the team of specialists assigned the task.[2] Turing's genius was undeniable, but the "eccentric" label was well deserved. He held up his pants with a string and wore a pajama top under his jacket instead of a shirt. He chained his tea mug to a radiator pipe with a combination lock. The sight of blood made him faint, so he shaved with an old electric razor, leaving him with a dark stubble that made him look ominous. A high-pitched, mechanical laugh, combined with a nervous stammer that frustration could turn into a snarl, added to the mad-scientist impression.

Although trained as a mathematician, Turing had a special interest in machines. In 1935, at age twenty-three, he had devised the *Universal Turing Machine*, "an imaginary device which established the possibilities and limitations for every computer which will ever exist, no matter how complex."[3] Of course, no computer did exist at that time, and so engineers and scientists shrugged off his paper as purely theoretical while most of Turing's fellow mathematicians viewed it as science fiction. Only time would bring recognition of the Universal Turing Machine as "the necessary bridge between the world of logic and the world in which people did things."[4] Alan Turing may not have developed the first computer, but his work made clear what a computer could be used for in the real world.

Although Turing was "disappointed by its reception," his paper on the Universal Turing Machine brought him to the attention of the British government.[5] Sometime between 1936 and 1938, he was approached to join the Government Code and Cypher School, Britain's top-secret code-breaking operation. The school was moved to suburban Bletchley Park near London, where Turing's involvement with the Nazis' Enigma machine began.

The British decoders' task was not much different from that of the Polish decoders. The method that the Poles had been using to determine the rotor settings would still work in theory. The increase in the stock of rotors, however, made the time necessary to come up with the settings much too long. Turing's team had to devise a way to make the procedure more efficient. They rose to the challenge.

Turing recognized that code breaking is a game of probabilities and elimination. He knew that the length of words and the frequency and repetition of letters are major clues. For instance, if they could determine what the first word of a Nazi transmission was likely to be, they would have a clue to the rotor positions. Suppose they determined that the word *Führer* occurred at the beginning (or end) of most messages. Its letters could be tracked as they changed when the rotors turned. As the day's messages were studied, a pattern might emerge that could help reveal the settings of the rotors. This was called the probable word method. Turing also studied rules of linguistic consistency in the German language. For example, *sch* is a common sequence of letters in German, but *jgt* is not a common sequence, if it exists at all.

Turing's team incorporated these rules into a new generation of Bombes. The new Bombes were based on electromagnetic relay switches used in automatic telephone exchanges. These relays could switch operations in a thousandth of a second. This vastly increased the mechanical speed of the Bombes.

While the new Bombes were being developed, the German Navy had actually increased its repertoire of Enigma rotors from five to eight. Top-secret documents recovered from captured German boats, however, provided enough information on the German operation of the Enigma machine to combat the improvement. At last, when the new Bombes were completed, and enough secret cipher data had been seized from German boats, the team at Bletchley Park could efficiently decode the German transmissions.

The decoding operation at Bletchley Park proved so spectacularly successful that the Enigma information they decoded was given the highest secret classification under the code name *Ultra*. The second half of 1941 saw sinkings by U-boats fall to half their previous number. British prime minister Winston Churchill received a daily packet of Ultra data, and Royal Air Force squadron leader Frederick Winterbotham observed that he "ran the war on it."[6] In the summer of 1941, when Churchill visited Bletchley, Turing was introduced to him as one of the leaders of the Ultra providers. Churchill called the code breakers "the geese who laid the golden eggs and never cackled."[7]

Some weeks after their meeting, Turing, who was in a constant state of agitation because of problems at Bletchley, leapfrogged the chain of command and wrote to Churchill directly. First he complained of a shortage of Wrens (members of the British women's navy auxiliary) to operate the Bombes. Then he expressed his disapproval of the threat that trained male decoding typists might be drafted into the military. He worried "that the importance of the work [of the code breakers] is not being impressed with sufficient force upon those outside authorities with whom we have to deal."[8]

Churchill responded immediately with an order to his chief staff officer: "ACTION THIS DAY: Make sure they have all they want on extreme priority and report to me that this has been done."[9]

In February 1942, the success of the Bletchley Park code breakers came to an abrupt end. Once again, the Germans altered the Enigma machine. The new machines featured a simple but devastating addition. The Germans added space for a fourth rotor in the Enigma machine. The Bombes that existed, even improved by the new telephone switchboard technology, simply did not have the capacity to handle the enormous increase in letter-per-keystroke possibilities.

By 1943, sinkings of Allied merchant ships were above their 1940–41 levels and the shipping situation was critical. The death toll among Allied merchant seamen was mounting and eventually it would total 50,000. For a short time, Ultra had provided speedy access to U-boat positions and movements. Now the British Admiralty was back in the dark.

There was pressure on the team at Bletchley. They needed a super-Bombe, a machine that could scan and decode with lightning speed. It would have to go through literally millions of coded letters and make instantaneous judgments about their patterns. To their knowledge, a machine with anything close to this kind of power had never been built.

The abstract solution came relatively easily to the Bletchley code breakers. The mechanics were more difficult. What available gadgetry could provide the speed needed? The answer was to use vacuum tubes similar to those in radios to power on-off switches with digital functions.

Dubbed *Colossus*, the new decoder went into production in February 1943. It was finished and began operating in December. Standing almost twice as tall as those who operated it, Colossus boasted four electrical switchboards, 2,400 vacuum tubes, and five punched-tape *scanners*. It could process 5,000 Enigma keystrokes per second. By the end of the war, a year and a half later, there were ten Colossus decoders in operation.

U-boat sinkings began falling off shortly after the first Colossus became operative. With Enigma transmissions now easily read, the movements of the German submarines were easily tracked. Allied corvettes and larger subchasers could zero in on them. Where once they had preyed on vulnerable merchant ships with impunity, the Nazi U-boats were now themselves the prey.

In creating Colossus, the Bletchley team had built more than just a superfast decoding machine, and more than a unique weapon of war. In fact, they had built an electronic digital computer.

The results of the Ultra produced by Colossus was "a decisive contribution to winning the war," according to U.S. general Dwight D. Eisenhower. U.S. general Douglas MacArthur confirmed its "supreme importance." And Churchill himself craved the intelligence the machine afforded him.[10]

This praise was not public knowledge. For decades, the accomplishments of Alan Turing and the other code breakers at Bletchley remained one of the most closely guarded government secrets of the twentieth century. Colossus and the other developments at Bletchley remained unknown until 1974.

Because of the secrecy, none of the code breakers was able to bask in the public glory of his success. Enduring the postwar obscurity was undoubtedly a burden for all the Bletchley code breakers. Alan Turing's obscurity, however, is especially troubling due to speculation that his achievements have remained little known because he was gay.

2
X=INSOLENCE

When Alan Mathison Turing was born on June 23, 1912, fifteen years after Oscar Wilde served two years in jail for violating laws against homosexuality, such laws were still being enforced in England—as they would be against Turing forty years later. Wilde had been Great Britain's most renowned playwright and poet. Turing would be considered the father of modern computer science, and the most prestigious prize in the field would be named after him. Intolerance of homosexuality destroyed both men.

Turing was born two years before the start of World War I, and signs of imminent strife already rocked Europe. In Great Britain, there were violent conflicts between labor and capital. In their battle for the vote, women suffragists staged hunger strikes and chained themselves to doorposts to block the halls of government. Ireland, under British rule, was on the verge of civil war. Prewar turmoil seized the British Isles.

Viewed through the filter of nostalgia from far-off India, however, the turmoil was not apparent. The British who governed India regarded England as a peaceful homeland filled with contented people. To them it was a safe haven from the daily dangers and violent upheavals of India.

Indians were rebelling against British rule. Muslims and Hindus were locked in an ongoing struggle.

Within each group, subgroups vied for power. Armed bands fought pitched battles and terrorized villages and farmers into paying them tribute. The level of violence was rising.

Alan Turing's father, Julius, assistant collector and magistrate for three rugged interior districts, had brought his bride to India in January 1908. Ethel Stoney Turing was born in India, where her father was a chief engineer of the Madras and Southern Mahratta Railway, but she grew up in Ireland. She was recovering from an unhappy love affair when she met Julius Turing aboard a cruise ship in the Orient. When it reached Japan, Julius invited her to dinner and whispered to the waiter, "Bring beer and keep on bringing beer until I tell you to stop."[1]

They married a few months later, on October 1, 1907, in Dublin. Their first child, John, was born at Conoor in India slightly less than a year later. By 1912, they were expecting another.

But India was becoming increasingly dangerous for English administrators and their families as violence against them grew. A bomb was thrown at Lord Charles Hardinge, the British viceroy of India, and the explosion knocked him off his elephant. The assassination attempt failed, but it made the Turings doubt the wisdom of raising children in India.

Alarmed by the possibility that events in Europe (war in the Balkans and between Italy and Turkey) might soon prevent travel to England, Julius and Ethel decided to leave while they could. Along with their three-and-a-half-year-old son, John, they set sail for England early in 1912. Shortly after their arrival, Alan Turing was born at Warrington Lodge, a nursing home in Paddington, London.

He was nine months old when his father returned to India. Six months later, Ethel rejoined Julius. Alan, barely a toddler, and John, not quite five years old, remained behind in England.

The Turings had placed their children in the custody of Colonel and Mrs. Ward, who lived in the town of St. Leonards-on-Sea. At different times, as many as eight other children inhabited the large house overlooking the ocean, including four of the Wards' daughters and three cousins of John and Alan Turing.

Colonel Ward and his wife believed in strict discipline, particularly for boys. World War I had broken out in Europe, Englishmen were fighting and dying by the tens of thousands, and war fever gripped Britain itself. The Wards, patriotic and militaristic by background and tradition, saw to it that John and Alan's playthings were toy guns and cannons and models of the heavily armored battleships known as dreadnoughts. The Wards were determined that the boys should grow up to be "real men."[2]

John rebelled against this and his younger brother, Alan, followed his lead. Alan refused to learn to fight back when bullied by other children, disdained war toys, and threw tantrums. In a letter to their mother in India, Mrs. Ward complained about their attitude. John, she wrote, was a hopeless bookworm.

But it was Alan who most disturbed the adults. By the time he was three years old, they already considered him willful, sloppy, and impudent. He had constant battles with Nanny Thompson, his nursemaid, and with Colonel and Mrs. Ward.

After Ethel Turing risked the dangerous journey through submarine-infested waters for a short visit to Britain, she wrote a letter to her husband describing her young son's behavior:

Alan will in a moment cry with rage and attempt to hold his breath, and in the next moment he will laugh at his tears, saying "Look at my big tears," and squeeze his eyes and say, "Ah" with his mouth wide open trying to squeeze out more tears for fun.[3]

His mother returned to India with this parting question, "You'll be a good boy, won't you?" Little Alan's answer was "Yes, but sometimes I shall forget."[4] Even John, who was himself considered rebellious, thought that "Alan was quite a nuisance."[5]

John was sent away to Hazelhurst, a small boarding school, in 1917. Alan, not yet five years old, was reunited with his mother. She had again risked sailing to England, this time to remain until the war's end while Alan's father stayed in India. Tensions between mother and son grew when she insisted that he regularly attend high Anglican church services with her. The incense tickled his nose, and he didn't like the aroma. "The church with the bad smells" was how he would always remember the cathedral.[6]

Even as a little boy, Alan seemed filled with contradictions. He was as bright as he was difficult. Nanny Thompson, marveled at "his integrity and his intelligence for a child so young."[7]

He taught himself to read in only three weeks, but words were not his greatest interest. Alan learned to recognize numbers even before he could identify letters of the alphabet. Large combinations of numbers fascinated him, and he would protest vigorously if he was studying a serial number on a lamppost and his mother or nursemaid tried to drag him away.

Still, he had his blind spots. It would be years before he could master long division. No matter how many times he was told, he could not memorize which was his left and which his right hand. Finally, frustrated, he painted a red mark on his left thumb. He called this "the knowing spot."[8]

Maps also fascinated him. The atlas that Alan asked for and received as a birthday present was his most prized possession. He studied it for hours on end.

When Alan was six, his father returned from India. He took his sons trout fishing. Alan quickly lost interest, and while his father and John were wading in the lake, he went off on his own to look for honey from wild bees. He observed the swarms of bees in flight and figured out from their flight paths where they would intersect. This, he calculated, was where they stored the honey. He was right, and he gathered enough honey for the family picnic.

He was right often enough to make others regard him as an annoying know-it-all. When his father used the phrase *flat as a pancake*, Alan sneered that "pancakes are generally rolled up."[9] He stated unequivocally that the fruit that Eve gave Adam in the Garden of Eden was a plum, not an apple. Even his mother thought he was unsociable.

Alan's parents went back to India after the war. He was again left with the spit-and-polish Wards while his brother John returned to the Hazelhurst School. The Wards deplored Alan's stubbornness and disobedience, and they wrote to his parents to complain. Alan had been teaching himself to ride a bicycle, pedaling around and around over their lawn, and when they called to him to stop and come indoors, he shouted back, "I can't get off until I fall off."[10]

Despite the strict environment, Alan's curiosity could not be contained. Every fact he stumbled upon gave rise to a question in his nine-year-old mind. *What makes water?* he wondered, and when he found out its composition, he wrote to his mother, asking "What makes the oxygen fit so tightly into the hydrogen to produce water?"[11] She could not answer his question.

At the beginning of 1922, six months before his tenth birthday, Alan was also enrolled at Hazelhurst. John was not exactly delighted to have him there and, as it turned out, with good reason. He was humiliated when Alan, four years younger, scored higher than he in a school-wide geography test. And he was furious when, during a school concert, his voice solo was disrupted by Alan choking with laughter. But John soon graduated from Hazelhurst, and from then on Alan was on his own with no big brother to torment—or to look after him.

There were only thirty-six boys at Hazelhurst, and Alan was possibly the least popular among them. He was awkward at sports and ran away from any ball that came his way. He was a complete dud at hockey, soccer, and cricket. Later in life, when he was an accomplished runner with Olympic ambitions, he would say that he got his start fleeing from the ball.

His marks were merely average, and he had what today would be called an "attitude problem." This did not endear him to his teachers any more than to his fellow students. He let it be known that his algebra teacher "gave a quite false impression of what is meant by x."[12] It was no wonder that Alan infuriated his teachers and that they considered him both lazy and insolent.

Throughout this time, in his contrary way, Alan was plunging into the study of science all on his own. He came across *Natural Wonders Every Child Should Know*, a book by Edwin Tenney Brewster, and it opened his eyes to a world he hadn't known existed. Alan focused initially on the sections dealing with biology and for the first time, in a roundabout way, learned about sex.

What he learned, however, left Alan puzzled. Eggs and such were all very well, but where did the original seed come from? He raised the question in a letter to his mother. Her answer spoke mystifyingly of birds and bees and counseled him "not to go off the rails."[13]

Alan was unenlightened, but his fascination with biology continued, and on his own he sought books to read. It was the beginning of a lifelong curiosity. Although he would be best known for his contributions to the then unknown field of computer science, his interest in organisms and groundbreaking work in biochemistry would continue right up to his death.

According to P. T. Saunders, who edited Turing's papers on biology, his earliest methods were "typical of all his work: his ability to identify a crucial problem . . . lack of interest in what others were doing . . . selection of an appropriate approach . . . ease with which he handled a wide range of techniques."[14] These qualities were evident from the beginning in young Alan's pursuit of a variety of scientific subjects. While he continued to study biology, he also became interested in the other sciences. In particular, he was fascinated by machines, or more accurately gadgets, and the way they worked.

He was not quite eleven years old when he constructed a fountain pen. Describing it in a letter to his mother, he explained that it had to be squeezed "to fill it" and then released so that "the ink is sucked up and it is full." The pen, however, was not an unqualified success. He complained, "When I press a little of the ink comes down, but it keeps on getting clogged."[15]

During the summer vacation of 1923, Alan and his brother, John, were entrusted by their absent parents to the Archdeacon Rollo Meyer and his wife. The archdeacon was a religious man, but Mrs. Meyer had a superstitious side. She took Alan to a church fair where a gypsy fortune teller predicted his future. Alan, the gypsy said, was going to be a great genius.

That autumn, Julius Turing resigned from the Indian Civil Service. However, to avoid tax on the large pension he would receive, he did not return to England. Instead, he and his wife moved to France, where Alan and his brother saw little of them except during vacation visits.

By now, however, Alan was used to having parents who distanced themselves from him. Besides, he had immersed himself in a new scientific interest: chemistry. Initially, his interest was sparked by Brewster's *Natural Wonders*, which proclaimed that "the life of any creature . . . is one long fight against being poisoned" and went on to discuss the effects of "the various *alkaloids,* such as *strychnine* and *atropin* and *cocaine.*"[16]

Alan's appetite was whetted for more knowledge of the workings of chemical substances, particularly poisons, including their interactions and effects on the biological systems of various life-forms. "Don't forget the science book I was to have," he wrote his parents in September of 1924. He also asked them for "the chemical name of cooking soda or the formula better still"[17] in order to understand better how it might change to carbon dioxide in the lungs. "With the help of the encyclopaedia," his mother would later recall, "he was trying to learn organic chemistry by himself (at twelve and a half)!"[18]

For Christmas that year, Alan received a chemistry set complete with a variety of basic substances, test tubes, and flasks. Soon he was spending all his free time brewing evil-smelling chemical mixtures and maintaining extensive files of notes on their interactions. The following summer, on a visit to his parents at their seaside home in France, he collected seaweed. He spent hours in the basement working on an experiment to extract iodine from it. Finally, he succeeded. Nevertheless, his mother worried. "I am sure," she told a friend, "that he will blow up himself and the house one day."[19]

He didn't. But Alan did go on to perform more and more advanced experiments in chemistry. Soon his pockets were filled with bits of paper on which he had scrawled formulas he had worked out. "I always seem to want to make things from the thing that is commonest in nature and with the least waste of energy," he wrote during his last year at Hazelhurst in March 1925.[20]

His teachers, however, were neither impressed nor pleased with Alan's obsession with science. The purpose of Hazelhurst was to prepare boys to pass the entrance examinations for the more advanced institutions they must attend if they were to later continue their education at the university level. His parents had always intended that Alan should do this, and he took it for granted that he would. However, the entrance examinations were keyed to Latin, Greek, literature, and a more classical education in general; the physical sciences were regarded as a distraction from these necessary subjects. Alan's spelling and grammar were appalling (and remained so throughout his life), and his instructors considered his focus on gadgetry and noxious chemical experiments to be the mark of an undisciplined mind.

Despite their opinion, in the spring of 1926, thirteen-year-old Alan passed the entrance examinations for Sherborne, a renowned three-century-old prep school for boys. He arrived there to join 400 schoolmates on May 3, 1926. A few days later, a group of them stuffed Alan into a wastepaper basket and vied with each other to kick it up and down the hall. His mother later recalled that from his very first letter she could tell that Alan "was hopelessly miserable."[21]

The misery of Alan Turing's adolescent school days, however, was just beginning.

3

A "HOPELESSLY MISERABLE" MISFIT

Sherborne was an English public school, which is equivalent to an American private school. Before the mid-nineteenth century, only the children of aristocrats could attend institutes like Sherborne. But when they began admitting any students whose families could afford to pay their fees, they became known as public schools. Profits from additional tuition fees, rather than any desire to equalize opportunity, were the reason for the change.

Around this time, the lax morals and wild behavior of the ruling classes were widely blamed on their schooling. The schools had become uncivilized. The boys were too wild, and flogging them only made them wilder. Discipline had to be enforced; their energy had to be channeled. And so organized exercise was introduced, marking the beginning of public school sports.

Mens sana in corpore sano, "a healthy mind in a healthy body," became the motto for English public schools. Athletic competition became a tradition, and then a hallowed tradition. It anchored the boys, it was said, and turned them into just the sort of men needed to run the affairs of the British Empire.

There were, however, some who believed the tradition a hollow one. Even though it regimented the boys, they argued, it stressed athletics and the body at the expense of studies and the mind. Despite these detractors, sports, especially cricket, hockey, and rugby football, were central to life at Sherborne.

Sports competition, however, was not the only tradition at Sherborne. There were also two disciplinary traditions that the older boys would inflict on delinquent underclassmen. They were birching, whipping a birch rod across the palms or buttocks; and fagging, inflicting a variety of torments, physical and mental, on younger boys who did not do well on the playing fields. Since Sherborne was a boarding school, there was no recourse from the bullying. The boy who did not fit in, who did not conform, was in for a very rough time. Alan Turing was such a boy.

He was prominent among the new arrivals at Sherborne from the first. When his journey there had been interrupted by a general strike that shut down railway service throughout Britain, young Alan had traveled the 60 miles (100 km) from Southampton, where the ferry had dropped him, to Sherborne by bicycle. Thirty years later, housemaster Geoffrey O'Hanlon would remember vividly "a somewhat untidy boy arriving during the Railway Strike, after making his way on a bicycle from Southampton . . . and reporting 'I am Turing.'"[1] At the time, the local newspaper also reported Alan's feat.

This brought him recognition and some admiration, but the admiration was short-lived. The Sherborne headmaster, Nowell Smith, assigned Alan living quarters at Westcott House. This was considered a more liberal environment than most because housemaster O'Hanlon, a bachelor in his forties, tried to keep a lid on the hazing of the younger boys. Whereas the school emphasized "ideas of authority and obedience," meant not only to maintain discipline over the boys, but also to teach them how to rule over others as upper-class Englishmen when they became adults, O'Hanlon "encouraged music and art."[2] When the head boy of Westcott House asked that the cyclist Alan Turing be appointed as his fag (a slang term for "servant"), O'Hanlon approved.

It was an honor, but it was soon undermined by Alan himself when he began performing chemistry experiments in his room. They gave off foul-smelling odors that offended the head boy and enraged Alan's other housemates. They got even with him by ganging up on him in the washroom and taking turns whacking him. Some mornings they forced him to take ice-cold showers. When he emerged from them, he often found his towel had been stolen. Once, some older boys trapped Alan and forcibly held him in a small space beneath the flooring of a Westcott House common room.

The usually easygoing housemaster, O'Hanlon, did not appreciate the vile chemical smells coming from Alan's room either. He may have valued art and music, but he was no more approving of science than the higher authorities of Sherborne. Headmaster Nowell Smith summed up the attitude: "It is only the shallowest mind that can suppose . . . scientific discovery brings us appreciably nearer to the solution of the riddles of the universe."[3] Housemaster O'Hanlon thought Alan was guilty of "trying to build a roof before he has laid the foundations" in his scientific experiments.[4] Still, Alan may have had no choice but to do it on his own. Instruction in science at Sherborne was limited to a grudging two hours a week, and for Alan it was pretty basic stuff.

Nothing set Alan apart so much as the attitude toward sports he brought with him to Sherborne. Competition among the school's houses in cricket, rugby football, and hockey was fierce. Alan not only played all of these games as badly as ever, letting down Westcott House and his housemates, but he made it obvious that he thought the games unimportant and didn't much care who won or how badly he did. In an environment where the boys bonded through sports, and team loyalties deepened into lifelong friendships, Alan's uncaring demeanor was viewed as treachery to ingrained English public school tradition. Nor did it help his standing with his fellow students when he got himself excused from contact sports and was allowed to take up golf instead.

He made no friends. The other boys called him "a drip" and teased him unmercifully.[5] In a way, the constant insults pained Alan more than the physical hazing. In defense, he adopted a supercilious pose. His quick comebacks to insults were usually intellectual put-downs. Naturally, these made him even less popular.

Alan was no more acceptable to his teachers than to his fellow students, and he was not much more successful with his classwork than with sports. During his first two years at Sherborne, he made it obvious that most of his teachers, and the subject matter they taught, bored him. One instructor in Latin and English wrote about Alan, "I can forgive his writing, though it is the worst I have ever seen, and . . . his . . . slipshod, dirty work . . . but I cannot forgive the stupidity of his attitude towards sane discussion on the New Testament."[6]

He had no particular interest in biblical studies or English literature, and his essays were marred—as they had been before he came to Sherborne—by atrocious spelling and grammatical errors. He failed Greek three times and was finally allowed to drop the class. His French teacher wrote that "his lack of interest is very depressing."[7]

His marks were generally bad, but not perhaps as bad as they should have been. He would infuriate some of his teachers by ostentatiously ignoring them during class all through the term and then scoring high grades on the finals by cramming at the last minute. Even the comparatively permissive housemaster O'Hanlon thought Alan behaved with "idleness and indifference."[8] The shortcomings he had developed prior to Sherborne definitely seemed to be hardening into lifelong bad habits there.

During his second year at Sherborne, Alan's interest in science propelled him into a new obsession: mathematics. It was, of course, taught at Sherborne, but Alan characteristically pursued it in much greater depth outside the classroom. When he showed his mathematics teacher, Mr. Randolph, some computations he had done on his own involving a complex formula for the inverse tangent function in trigonometry, Randolph told the other masters that Alan was "a genius."[9]

Being "a genius," however, did not excuse Alan for violating Sherborne's standards for dress and neatness. The school took pride in the appearance of its students, and few of them let the school down as badly as Alan did. He was careless to the point of slovenliness and there were those—teachers and students alike—who said he was just plain dirty.

Unfortunately, Alan had an oily complexion. His hair fell flatly over his forehead, and no amount of combing could pin it back. This gave his head the appearance of being flat on top, rather than rounded, a characteristic that in those days was thought to indicate a low intelligence. When fastening his shirts and jackets, he habitually mismatched the buttons and buttonholes, giving him a foolish, lopsided appearance. His shirttails often hung outside his pants, and when he was deep in thought his shoulders hunched up as if he suffered from some deformity. His lifelong stammer was already quite noticeable.

Working on his own projects, not necessarily having to do with his classwork, Alan would become so engrossed that he would move his pen over his clothing and over his face and hands, leaving a trail of ink.

This became an ongoing joke in one of his classes. The teacher would repeatedly get a laugh at Alan's expense by greeting him with "Ink on your collar again, Turing." The phrase followed him after class when the other boys would jeer it at him over and over again: "Ink on your collar again, Turing."[10]

Cruel as this was, Alan usually managed to shrug it off by losing himself in science and mathematics. He also focused on the game of chess, and although he had nobody to play games with, he spent countless hours working out chess problems by himself. Eventually chess became more than a game to him; it became a useful metaphor for explaining his theories regarding the nature and limitations of computers.

During Alan's second year at Sherborne, in the autumn of 1927, a new teacher came to the school. His name was A. H. Trelawny Ross, and he taught Latin and English. He was a stickler for form and spelling. Also, he believed that Germany had lost World War I because it esteemed "science and materialism" over "religious thought and observance."[11] From the first, Alan and Mr. Ross were on a collision course.

When Mr. Ross delivered lectures on how "as democracy advances, manners and morals recede," Alan surreptitiously worked out algebra problems under his desk. The teacher caught him and, furious, gave him failing grades in both English and Latin. Alan had fallen "ludicrously behind," according to an evaluation by Mr. Ross. With it, he included a page smeared with ink as an example of Alan's messy work.[12]

The headmaster agreed, writing to Alan's parents that he was "anti-social" and "the kind of boy who is bound to be rather a problem in any kind of school."[13] Still, Alan did well in his mathematics classes and in those science courses Sherborne had to offer. And he continued with these interests outside class.

Mr. Ross sneered at these activities, referring to the

scientific subjects as "low cunning." He snorted that Alan's "room smells of mathematics," adding that he should "Go out and fetch a disinfectant spray."[14]

Despite such judgments, Alan continued going his own way. In the summer of 1928, he was not promoted to the next grade. He was, however, allowed to take an advanced course in mathematics. This led to an interest in the work of Albert Einstein, the greatest physicist of the twentieth century. On his own, Alan began reading Einstein's works and making notes on what he read. In a book of these notes that he gave to his mother, Alan observed that "Einstein here throws doubt" on "*Euclid's axioms.*"[15]

His brother, John, thought this typical of Alan. "If you ventured on some self-evident proposition, as for example that the earth was round," he observed, "Alan would produce a great deal of incontrovertible evidence to prove that it was almost certainly flat."[16] In fact, though, Alan's comment showed a grasp of one of Einstein's key points—that space is not absolute as Euclid (the ancient Greek mathematician who first framed the rules of geometry around 300 B.C.) presents it. Einstein proposed that space and time are not independent of each other, and the combination of the two is curved in a way that Euclid didn't foresee.

While many leading mathematicians were still struggling with Einstein's theory of relativity, Alan had comprehended one of its most important points. Perhaps it was typical of the boy that what he appreciated most about Einstein was his unwillingness to be bound by so-called scientific truth. It was this that had led to the theories that *The Times* of London had termed "an affront to common sense." The "affront" had, as Alan well knew, revolutionized the science of physics.[17]

Challenging such *truths* came naturally to Alan. It was part of his nature to question generally accepted concepts, and this skepticism would be typical of his work throughout his life. He also admired Einstein's emphasis on an "operational approach" to physics, which focused on the practical and mechanical as opposed to the purely abstract.[18]

Reading Einstein affected Alan like champagne. He was intoxicated and inspired to scrawl his own ideas. "Ways of measuring are really conventions," he wrote. "You modify your laws to suit your method of measurement."[19] As much a rephrasing of Einstein as an original thought, it was nevertheless an idea that would resurface some years later when Alan conceived the Universal Turing Machine.

Alan focused on Einstein, and on science and mathematics generally, as a way of coping with his unhappy situation at Sherborne. Failing grades and unsympathetic teachers, awkwardness at sports and the insults and hazing by his fellow students, an unfortunate stammer and the low self-image reflected by his slovenliness and defensive arrogance—these were heavy burdens for a teenage boy to bear. But they were not his only burdens, and immersing himself in his self-assigned studies was not the only way he dealt with them.

Sometime during his first two years at Sherborne, according to Alan Turing's biographer, Andrew Hodges, young Alan realized that he "was drawn by love and desire" to members of "his own sex." Of course, this set him apart from the other boys, who, as might be expected in an all-male teenage environment, were caught up in an ongoing discussion about women and sex. The rules of the school forbade such talk, the headmaster warning the boys against "swearing and coarse jokes and vulgar innuendoes."[20] But the warning was ignored, and the boys' fascination with the topic was too strong for the rules to be enforced. Alan, however, did not participate in such conversations.

He was only vaguely aware that there might be

homosexual activity among any of the other boys. The school, however, was constantly on guard to prevent it. When *The Loom of Youth* by Alec Waugh, a book dealing with same-sex love, circulated around the school, the headmaster forbade Sherborne students to read it (which, of course, didn't stop them). In the same spirit of prevention, Alan's nemesis, Mr. Ross, prohibited boys from studying together without a teacher present lest their curiosity lead them down forbidden paths.

Sherborne dealt with sex generally by seeing to it that the boys took frequent cold showers. Alan managed to distract his own secret desires in another way: he began going on long, solitary runs.

Running was a safety valve releasing the energy he was forbidden to release in keeping with his feelings. Actually, Alan was still quite innocent, even naïve. He had only a superficial comprehension of sex, and he understood his own needs even less. He was confused. He felt there was nobody he could confide in. He had no friends.

And then he met Christopher Morcom.

4
"GOOD NIGHT, SWEET PRINCE"

Christopher Morcom was not attracted to males in the same way Alan Turing was, so the relationship between them was never physical. Yet it evolved into a friendship so deep that love may be the only word to describe it. It was as short as it was sweet, and it was the most important relationship in Alan's life.

"He made everyone else seem so ordinary" was how Alan characterized his feelings for Christopher.[1]

At Sherborne, however, it was Alan who stood out and Christopher who blended in with the other students. Unlike Alan, he conformed. It came easily to him, for like most of us, he liked to be liked. He was by nature amiable, did not flaunt his considerable intelligence, and avoided confrontations.

A year older than Alan and one grade ahead of him in school, Christopher was slender, wiry, and small for his age. He had pale-blond hair and very light skin. His face was elongated, his demeanor sensitive. In contrast to Alan, he always got high grades, had won school prizes, was a leading candidate for university scholarships, and was highly praised by his teachers.

Although he contracted frequent colds that kept him out of school for weeks at a time, Christopher appeared energetic and was not viewed as sickly by his schoolmates, nor by Alan. What neither they nor Alan knew, however, was that Christopher had for many years suffered from tuberculosis. Triggered by ordinary colds, flare-ups of the disease were progressively more severe.

Christopher and Alan became friendly at the beginning of the autumn 1927 school term. They were initially drawn to each other by a mutual interest in science and mathematics. Each recognized in the other a keenness and a desire to explore the mysteries of the universe, a desire that remained unawakened in most of the other boys at Sherborne. They excelled in this pursuit—Alan arrogantly so, Christopher with modesty.

For Alan there was another aspect of the attraction, but Christopher set clear limits. "I have some very definite ideas of right and wrong," he told Alan.[2] He understood that Alan's feelings went beyond friendship, but he neither responded to them nor let them stand in the way of their relationship.

When it came to science, each respected the other and took his ideas very, very seriously. Alan introduced Christopher to the theories of Einstein. Christopher impressed on Alan the need to be thorough in the chemistry experiments they did together, and the importance of follow-through. He even managed to convince Alan to try to make his handwriting neater. Thanks to Alan, Christopher explored mathematics and science in much greater depth and learned to look at them nontraditionally. Thanks to Christopher, Alan widened his horizons and began to develop some social skills.

Christopher had studied music and was an accomplished piano player. He introduced Alan to the great composers. He brought Alan with him to musical get-togethers organized by one of the teachers who played recordings of Beethoven, Bach, and Vivaldi to acquaint students with the great symphonic works. At these musical Sunday afternoons, Alan, for the first time, began to form tenuous relationships with some of the other boys.

For the first time he had a friend, and this gave Alan a sense of self-worth. It built his confidence, and made him less defensive, which in turn made him less aggressive. Also, prodded gently by Christopher, he began to take more pains with his appearance. While the ink smears never altogether disappeared from his skin and clothing, Alan became more careful about such matters as matching buttons with the proper buttonholes, tying shoelaces securely enough that he would not trip over them, and tucking in his shirttails. He even attempted to keep his hair combed back, although his habit of running his fingers through it when he was preoccupied undermined the effort.

Despite this, the change in Alan was pronounced. Even his parents noticed it and began criticizing his demeanor less and valuing his talents more. "At home," his mother would write of this period in contrast to the family's past doubts about him, "we regarded Alan as the family encyclopaedia; he seemed to have the answers to all our scientific queries."[3]

At Sherborne, the other boys stopped picking on Alan quite so much. Partly this was due to the effects of Christopher's influence on him, but there was another reason. Alan's running had begun to attract attention and even some admiration.

He had started to run as a way of dealing with feelings and impulses he did not know how to handle. There was nobody he could talk to about them, so Alan ran alone. He ran to the point of exhaustion because there was no other release for the energy they created. His stride was wide, but he ran flat-footed, and this made him look awkward. He lacked the acceleration for the quick sprint needed to win most races. However, because he had pushed himself to run longer and longer distances, he had developed the marathoner's endurance and with it an impressive swiftness over the long course.

Some of the racing competitions between Sherborne houses were distance events. Soon Alan was beating all comers in these longer contests. In the shorter team-relay races, according to another Westcott House boy, Alan became a "useful forward," unbeatable in rainy weather when his flat-footed gait gave him a substantial edge over the others running in the mud.[4]

Competing against other boys, let alone winning, was something new for Alan. He had always been a loner and gone his own way with little concern for doing better than anyone else. Success awakened his competitive instinct, and he recognized an element of it in his deepening relationship with Christopher.

"Chris's work was always better than mine," he wrote, "because . . . he was very thorough. . . . He never neglected details, and . . . very seldom made arithmetical slips." Alan added that "Chris always had a delightful pride in his performances and I think it was this that excited one's competitive instinct to do something which might fascinate him and which he might admire." Yet, Alan concluded with what seemed wonderment, "Chris always seemed to me very modest."[5]

Wanting to impress his friend, Alan calculated pi to thirty-six decimal places. To do this, he used his own previous calculations for the inverse tangent function. This and similar feats led one of his teachers to report that "he thinks very rapidly and is apt to be brilliant." But he added that Alan was still "unsound in some of his work."[6] And although Christopher was impressed by Alan's often dazzling mathematical feats, there was never any real competition between them as to grades. Christopher's marks were among the highest in the school, whereas Alan was just beginning to pull his grades up to an acceptable level.

Their relationship was not always confined to their mutual intellectual interests, and it was not always so serious. Brilliant as Christopher was, he had his playful side. Together with Alan, he was quite capable of mixing chemicals in the interest of executing boyish pranks. Once they climbed a railway trestle and when a train passed under it they dropped rocks into the funnel of the steam engine. One ricocheted and hit a stoker sitting in the cab. On another occasion they filled balloons with helium and propelled them so that they would drop on a nearby girls' academy. And, together with a third boy, they wrote a comedy skit. Christopher had intended to set it to music but never got around to it.

Perhaps he was sidetracked by one of his frequent bouts with illness. At such times, he was whisked away from Sherborne to his home. During such absences, Alan and he wrote many letters to each other. In keeping with the public school custom of calling boys by their last names, they addressed each other as "Dear Morcom" and "Dear Turing."[7]

They wrote about problems in chemistry and physics and mathematics, exchanging ideas and theories, making suggestions for experiments, and reporting the results. The experiments concerned such problems as how to measure the resistance of air as a body passed through it, and observations on the friction caused by water compared to other liquids. They recommended to each other articles and books dealing with physics, and particularly with relativity. They discussed plans for a reflecting telescope 20 feet (6 m) long.

Following Christopher's lead, Alan became interested in astronomy and then fascinated by it. The plans for the telescope were only the tip of the iceberg for him. In 1929, he read two books by Sir Arthur S. Eddington: *Internal Constitution of the Stars* and *The*

Nature of the Physical World. They dealt with quantum physics, mathematics, and Einstein's theories of relativity and gravity—all as they pertained to the stars and to the universe.

Even as Alan was reading, scientists were finding confirmation of Eddington's thesis, backed up by Einstein's theories. Mathematical computations of telescopic observations verified that the galaxies of the universe were moving away from the astronomers who observed them at a velocity proportional to their distances. Scientists quickly realized that this observation was characteristic of an expanding universe.

Alan and Christopher realized this too. The implications were mindboggling. If the universe was expanding, then science's conception of it must expand as well. There was the possibility of countless new galaxies, of endless space, and even—the idea took Alan's breath away—of other universes, countless other universes. Christopher tried to rein in his friend's imaginings without success. "[We] usually didn't agree," Alan would remember, "which made things much more interesting."[8]

The boys were obsessed with stars and galaxies and universes. The heavens had opened up before them and, in Alan's mind at least, they were limitless. So too, it seemed, was their interest in them. They had a French class together, and during it they used to slip each other notes arguing about astronomy. The notes were in French and were sometimes addressed "Cher ami"—"Dear friend." One was scrawled on the back of a class paper done by Alan on which the teacher had noted, "Nine wrong genders. . . . Very poor." Alan kept these notes and treasured the memory of a night when Christopher "grasped me with his big hand and took me out to see the stars."[9]

Despite his ongoing problems with grammar and spelling in English and French, Alan's overall grades improved. He moved up one level, and this allowed him to take many classes with Christopher. Both boys shone in mathematics, and the reports to Alan's parents were for the first time a source of pride—particularly to his father. In the summer of 1929, Alan was given permission to take the examination for the Higher School Certificate, a first step on the road to university, and he began studying for it. Christopher had long been eligible to take the test.

Christopher scored high marks on the examination, but Alan did only middling well. The examiner in mathematics for the Higher School Certificate noted that Alan "showed an unusual aptitude . . . for discovering methods which would at once shorten or illumine the solutions." However, he added that Alan lacked the patience to verify his computations "and his handwriting was so bad that he lost marks frequently—sometimes because his work was definitely illegible."[10]

Although his sloppy handwriting was fairly ingrained by now, Alan was inspired by Christopher to try to improve his work. Christopher, eighteen years old, intended to compete for a scholarship to Trinity College at Cambridge University. Alan, though a year younger, was distressed at the thought of losing his only friend, so he decided to try for the scholarship as well.

Trinity was the center of science and mathematics at Cambridge, and Cambridge was England's leading scientific university. Indeed, where science was concerned, it was one of the top institutions in the world. Boys who were thinking of going there were encouraged to visit first and acquaint themselves with the university. On December 6, 1929, Alan and Christopher took the train to London, where they were to meet a schoolmate who would drive them from there to Cambridge.

First, though, they stopped off in London to lunch

with Christopher's mother, a sculptor, who had a studio there. Alan and Mrs. Morcom got on very well. Indeed, their relationship would be a warm one until her death in 1941.

At Cambridge, the boys were on their own, free of the restrictions of Sherborne and of parental supervision for perhaps the first time. They looked over the school and its grounds, they played cards, and they went to the famous Observatory. They dressed in evening clothes for dinner in the great hall of Trinity College. Christopher checked Alan to make sure his buttons and tie and cuff links were all where they were supposed to be and were securely fastened.

Five days after they returned from Cambridge, on December 18, the *Times* of London published a list of those who had won scholarships to colleges and universities, including Trinity. Christopher's name was among them. Alan's was not.

Soon afterward the boys parted, each going his separate way for Christmas vacation with his family. Christopher wrote Alan, wishing him a "Happy Christmas" and informing him that he was "making a spectrograph."[11] Alan, in turn, decided to construct a model of the heavens that would show the constellations and fixed stars. He used an old, round lampshade—a glass globe of the type dating back to the gaslight era. In the wee hours of the morning he would get out of bed and go outside to look at the stars so that he might position them on the globe with the accuracy of his own personal observation.

Christopher wrote Alan about a comet he had spotted. "I wonder if you will be able to get hold of a telescope to look for it," he suggested.[12] Alan did indeed locate the comet and then proceeded to chart its course. When vacation was over, he brought his graph and the glass globe with the constellations marked on it back to Sherborne to show Christopher.

A few weeks later, on February 6, 1930, Alan and Christopher went to a singing concert at Sherborne. Much later that night, Christopher had a severe tubercular attack. An ambulance had to be called, and he was rushed to a hospital in London. His condition deteriorated. He was operated on twice during the next six days, but the operations were of no use. At noon on February 13, his heart failed and Christopher Morcom died.

Alan Turing lost his beloved and only friend.

5 TO KNOW THYSELF

Christopher's death affected Alan deeply. Early in 1930, he wrote to Ethel Turing:

I feel sure that I shall meet Morcom again somewhere and that there will be some work for us to do together . . . as I believed there was for us to do here. Now that I am left to do it alone I must not let him down but put as much energy into it, if not as much interest, as if he were still here. If I succeed I shall be more fit to enjoy his company than I am now.[1]

After Christopher's funeral, Alan also wrote a letter of condolence to his friend's mother. Mrs. Morcom was touched by the depth and sincerity of Alan's grief, and as a result, she invited him to join the family—herself, her husband, and Christopher's brother Rupert—on a vacation trip to Gibraltar. The trip had originally been planned to include Christopher, and now Alan would be taking his place.

It affirmed the closeness of the evolving relationship between Alan and the Morcoms, Mrs. Morcom in particular. He may have played some part in their decision to provide the money for an annual science prize at Sherborne to be presented to the boy whose work showed the greatest originality. But whether or not he had anything to do with the establishment of the Christopher Morcom Prize for Natural Science, Alan's devotion to Christopher's memory made him determined to win it.

His grief concentrated his energies. He had for some time been working on the interaction of certain chemicals, and the result of his efforts was his entry for the 1930 Morcom Prize, "The Reaction of Sulphates and Iodates in Acid Solution."[2] One of the competition's judges, A. J. P. Andrews, commented:

I first realized what an unusual brain Alan had when he presented me with a paper on the reaction between iodic acid and sulphur dioxide. . . . He had worked out the mathematics of it in a way that astonished me.[3]

Andrews added, "I have always thought Alan and his friend Christopher Morcom were the two most brilliant boys I have ever taught."[4]

Winning the Morcom Prize in 1930 took a great deal of Alan's energy, but not all of it. With Christopher gone, he ran longer and harder than ever. When he came in first in the steeplechase race among Sherborne houses, his housemates cheered him. This was a welcome contrast to their treatment of him during his earlier years at Sherborne. But if he was no longer an outcast, neither had he made any friendships to replace his relationship with Christopher. Rather wistfully, he wrote to his mother, "It never seems to have occurred to me to make other friends besides Morcom."[5]

Alan did keep up a correspondence with an ex-roommate named Matthew Blamey, but they never really became close. In mid-1930 he wrote Blamey, "I have started learning German," adding, "I may be made to go to Germany sometime." He didn't do too well at German, though. His teacher noted that Alan "does not seem to have any aptitude for languages."[6] Still, his German did improve, and it would stand him in good stead during the war when the Enigma messages would have to be decoded into German first, and then into English.

One reason Alan struggled with German may have been that his mind was elsewhere at the time. In the somewhat quirky way of his particular genius, Alan's study of Einstein's theories had focused him on an earlier development in physics known as the *Foucault pendulum*, which demonstrated the rotation of the earth. Einstein's theory of relativity raised questions about the relation of Foucault's work to "the stars," and to "the disposition of the heavens" themselves.[7] It was questions such as these, raised by Einstein himself, that made Alan take a second look at Foucault.

Jean-Bernard-Léon Foucault was a mid-nineteenth-century French physicist who had started out as a doctor. In the 1840s, he began a series of investigations of light and heat. In 1850, he established that light travels slower in water than in air. Subsequently he measured the speed of light, an accomplishment that would be central to the formation of Einstein's theories, and eventually to the development of space travel. He first demonstrated the Foucault pendulum in Paris in 1851.

It was a simple demonstration with profound implications. The pendulum consisted of a 62-pound (28-kg) iron ball suspended by a 220-foot (67-m) steel wire. A mechanism similar to a clock spring swung the pendulum in an arc with the regularity of a metronome. At the furthest point of the arc in one direction, Foucault visualized a straight line from the top of the wire to the iron ball. He did the same at the furthest point of the arc in the other direction. Then he conceived a third line joining the bottom points of the two lines to form a triangle perpendicular to the ground. If no outside forces influenced the pendulum, this triangle was the plane through which the pendulum would always pass during its constant rhythmic motion. On the floor under the pendulum he drew a straight line that corresponded to the bottom line of the triangle, and so to the arc in which the pendulum would swing.

Now something very strange happened. As the pendulum swung back and forth, the line traced by the arc of the pendulum clearly appeared to diverge from the line marked earlier on the floor. However, *neither the arc of the pendulum, nor its speed had changed!* It was the floor of the exhibition hall that was moving under the pendulum as the earth rotated on its axis. Foucault had isolated the effects of the earth's spin.

Almost eighty years later, this was basic physics. Even at Sherborne, where science took a back seat to other courses of study, schoolboys had learned about Foucault's pendulum early in their education. Nevertheless, Alan was intrigued by the questions raised by Einstein. Why exactly was it that "the pendulum kept its place fixed relative to the distant stars" regardless of the earth's rotation? "Why should there be an absolute standard of rotation" that agreed with the arrangement of the cosmos?[8] With typical hubris, Alan decided not to accept on faith the implications behind the questions, but rather to test the premises for himself.

He waited for a sunshiny Sunday when the other boys at Westcott House were either at chapel, off on long walks, or playing sports. Alone in the residence, Alan assembled the parts of a Foucault's pendulum he had made and strung it from the ceiling over the stairwell. He then began confirming for himself that the pendulum maintained its motion and position while the earth beneath it rotated. He was still recording his observations when the other boys of Westcott House began arriving home.

They were flabbergasted by the contraption Alan had set up. When the teachers and other members of the staff heard about it, they came to see for themselves and were deeply impressed by Alan's attempt to answer questions raised by Einstein himself. That he never succeeded in answering those questions didn't change the fact that Alan was now the center of attention at Sherborne. The recognition of his resourcefulness and budding genius now blotted out the memory of his careless work.

This was reinforced the following year, 1931, when Alan once again won the Morcom Prize. This time, however, it was only one of a handful of honors bestowed on him. Chief among them was a major scholarship to King's College at Cambridge University that gave him eighty pounds a year—twice the amount an unemployed British worker would get from the government dole during those difficult Depression years of the 1930s. The previous year, Alan had failed to win a Cambridge scholarship where Christopher succeeded, and that had been a bitter pill to swallow. Now he felt redeemed. Icing on the cake was provided by Sherborne when it awarded him the King Edward VI Gold Medal for Mathematics upon his graduation, while Westcott House gave him yet another scholarship.

During his last days at Sherborne, Alan had two experiences with a system of discipline—caning—that during most of his years there he had managed to avoid. He was now at the top of the pecking order, and it was his traditional prerogative to beat with a cane those younger boys whose behavior called for punishment. One such incident is described by one of these boys in a letter to Turing's biographer Andrew Hodges:

"I said . . . 'Turing, you look a disgusting sight.' . . . I tactlessly said it a second time. He took offense and told me to stay there and wait for him. . . . He duly reappeared with a cane, told me to bend over and gave me four."[9]

Alan's senior status gave him the responsibility for disciplining another boy, Victor Beuttell, who was three years younger than he. Victor frequently got into scrapes calling for punishment, but when Alan found out that Victor had been beaten so harshly for a previous infraction that his spine was permanently injured, he shelved his cane. For the first time, he thought seriously about the English public school practice of caning and questioned it. The answer he arrived at put him in opposition to caning and other forms of physical punishment for the rest of his life.

Despite this conclusion, Alan took a British Army Officer Training Corps course at Knightsbridge barracks before arriving at Cambridge. Although previously Alan had never been good at any sports except running, he now demonstrated the necessary strength and endurance to qualify as a reserve officer. He did particularly well in drill and tactics. The experience bolstered his confidence as he began his studies at Cambridge.

Cambridge University is one of the most hallowed and prestigious institutions in the world. It traces its beginnings to the year 1209, when a group of students from Oxford gathered there to continue their education. Its formal incorporation as a university took place in 1571. From 1669 through 1701, Isaac Newton was a professor of mathematics at Cambridge, and it was there that he evolved his most important theories. From Newton's time onward, mathematics has always been preeminent among the courses of study offered by the university. Among those who studied there a generation before Alan Turing were two of the world's greatest mathematicians, Alfred North Whitehead and Bertrand Russell, who met at Cambridge and subsequently coauthored the *Principia Mathematica*, one of the most important works in the history of mathematics. Without doubt, Cambridge was the ideal place for Alan to pursue his interest in mathematics and physics and to develop his talents.

He arrived there in October 1931. Nineteen years old, his features had already matured into those of the man he would be. With his sloping forehead, the pronounced forward thrust of his jaw, and the heavy, dark, beetling eyebrows that seemed to come together over the bridge of his nose, he was striking, but quite unhandsome. Together with his shambling manner, casual attention to dress, and high-pitched stammer, he presented an image to Cambridge that had an effect similar to the one he had on Sherborne as a boy. During those early days at Cambridge, he did not make any new friends.

As if to compensate, and perhaps spurred on by his success in the Officer Training Corps, Alan joined the college Boat Club. To everyone's surprise, for he looked anything but athletic, he made the King's College rowing team. This was a highly prized accomplishment. The annual Cambridge-Oxford competition is the oldest boat race in the world, and a competent oarsman was always a valued asset at Cambridge.

Alan was competent, but he was not a part of the close-knit athletic clique that reigned over the Boat Club. His fellow oarsmen granted his ability but regarded him as an egghead. Although Alan would continue to row during his years at Cambridge, he would always be considered a loner rather than one who fit in with the rest of the crew. He would always be more comfortable working off his energy with long, solitary runs than conforming to the ways of a team.

There was, of course, justification for the egghead label. It wasn't just that Alan was smart. It was also that he couldn't seem to control his arrogance in proving just how smart he was. There was, for instance, his disrespectful attitude toward recognized leaders in the field of mathematics. One of these was a much admired Polish theorist named Sierpinski. Alan wrote his mother about Sierpinski as follows:

"I pleased one of my lecturers . . . the other day by producing a theorem which he found had previously only been proved by one Sierpinski, using a rather difficult method. My proof is quite simple, so Sierpinski is scored off"—by which Alan meant that the Polish mathematician's reasoning was inferior to his own.[10]

While mathematics was Alan's main intellectual focus at this time, it was not his only one. He renewed his old interest in biology with a self-assigned experiment involving the interbreeding of drosophila, or fruit flies. The experiment had more to do with genetics than math. He identified one fly in particular as "Humphrey," and charted key characteristics of his descendants.[11]

Alan was midway through the experiment at vacation time when he was scheduled to visit his parents' home. Not wanting to abandon his work, he packed up the fruit flies in test tubes and incorporated the box of tubes into his luggage. When he unpacked, however, he found that the fruit flies had escaped the tubes. Humphrey's progeny had bred promiscuously, and there was no way to confine them to the suitcase. They swarmed over his parents' home and were a constant annoyance there for many weeks. His parents were not amused.

The impulsiveness that had led Alan to breed fruit flies was typical of him. He frequently acted on a whim. When he learned that his idol, Einstein, played the violin, he traveled to London and bought a second-hand instrument. He decided to master it on his own rather than take lessons. Alan always preferred to work things out for himself. Eventually, he took a great deal of pleasure in his playing, and he kept it up throughout his life.

During his years at Cambridge and thereafter, Alan kept up a correspondence with Christopher's mother, partly because he could not let go of his dead friend. When Chris had been dead three years, Alan commemorated the anniversary by writing Mrs. Morcom to say "I shall [be] thinking of Chris and of you tomorrow. I am sure that he is as happy now as he was when he was here."[12]

The thought seemed at odds with Alan's usual avoidance of spirituality. Scientific by nature, he was skeptical of ideas that did not have a logical foundation. He regarded daily school chapel as designed to put one "in a state of semi-coma." And yet, according to one who knew him well during his years at university, "within the framework of his science, he believed in the great order of things."[13]

Logic may have ruled his life, but Alan was not immune to the popular emotions of his time. During the 1930s, England was in bad shape and the rest of Europe was in worse. Unemployment in Great Britain was still widespread, and a government dole was all that stood between many working-class families and starvation. A general strike had pushed the government into enacting relief measures, but there was no end to the Depression in sight.

Meanwhile, fascism had ruled Italy for over ten years and was on the horizon in Spain. Germany had fallen into the hands of the Nazis and seemed bent on solving its own Depression by conquering its neighbors, plundering them, and eventually dragging Europe into war. The vast Soviet Union was in the iron grip of Bolshevism and was actively exporting its philosophy with the help of Communist Party cells in Great Britain and elsewhere. British socialists, caught between fascism and communism, and lacking the political clout to enact reform measures that might alleviate the Depression, concentrated their efforts on building a peace movement.

At Cambridge there was a strong antiwar tradition among students and some teachers even though the university administration frowned upon such protest. During World War I, when the famous mathematician and philosopher Bertrand Russell was already recognized as one of the world's great thinkers, he was fired from his lecture post at Cambridge for his antiwar activities and imprisoned for six months. Now, with the horrors of that war fresh in memory, a conviction that the carnage had been in vain gained credence among idealistic young people. Russell was regarded as a hero, if not a martyr, and the peace movement became a crusade with roots in the student body and faculty of the university.

In English politics, however, there grew vocal opposition to the spread of fascism, nazism, and communism throughout Europe. It was expressed in saber-rattling speeches and calls for a military buildup. Winston Churchill, an outspoken politician who was to become Great Britain's prime minister during World War II, was identified as a warmonger by many peace activists. The demands by Churchill and his political allies to rebuild England's fighting capacity, particularly its fleet of naval warships and artillery, were viewed by antiwar idealists as a distraction, perhaps a calculated distraction, from the nation's ongoing problems of unemployment.

Cambridge was split on these issues and feelings ran high. Inevitably, Alan had to take sides. His humanism and his vision of an orderly scientific program to deal with the ongoing economic crisis tipped the balance for Alan in favor of the peace movement. He wrote his mother that "I have joined an organization called the Anti-War Council. . . . Its program is principally to organize strikes among munitions and chemical workers when government intends to go to war. It [raises] a . . . fund to support the workers who strike. . . ."[14]

Together with other Cambridge King's College students opposing an arms buildup, Alan took part in parades and demonstrations. These attracted a wide variety of participants ranging from Quakers, Christian pacifists, and those who believed in the nonviolence of the Indian leader Mohandas K. Gandhi, to trade unionists, socialists, and communists. Alan had very little in common with many of them and little sympathy for many of their views.

As far as his politics were concerned, he was (for those days) a middle-of-the-road liberal. He believed strongly in individual liberty and at the same time thought that the economic system needed organization and controls. To run society by scientific planning seemed a sensible idea to him. But at the same time, he had read and liked the 1932 satire *Brave New World* by Aldous Huxley and understood the fear that science could regiment people.

If it was not consistent for one who had gone out of his way to take military training to join the peace movement, neither was Alan any more consistent in his views on other social and political problems. Always, he was unwilling to twist the evidence in the interest of his politics. Confronted by facts, he was always willing to change his views. He never hesitated to loose his high-pitched cackling laugh at his own opinions when the truth disagreed with them.

Shortly after Alan participated in a protest against a film called *Our Fighting Navy*, which he characterized as "blatant militarist propaganda," he went on a skiing vacation to Germany and Austria. Hitler's Nazis had come to power, and there were swastikas everywhere.

While Alan's group was not itself molested, they heard stories of other student groups, particularly those with Jews among them, being beaten by Nazi thugs. One of the German skiers who shepherded Alan's group was an ardent Nazi. One day Alan saw one of his countrymen bidding the Nazi farewell with the words "Heil Hitler" accompanied by the Nazi salute. "You shouldn't have said that," Alan told the young Englishman. [15]

Back at Cambridge, Alan became aware of an influx of German-Jewish professors who had been driven out of Germany by the Nazis. His readings in scientific journals told him that large numbers of persecuted Jewish scientists were fleeing Hitler's thugs. Awareness of the Nazi threat soon made Alan turn away from pacifist activities.

One Nazi outrage that shocked the world had personal relevance to Alan. This was the assassination, ordered personally by Hitler, of Ernst Röhm and the killing of some eighty-seven upper-echelon members of the SA (the German stormtroopers known as Brownshirts). Röhm and other leaders of the SA were homosexuals. Hitler had instructed the head of the Prussian Gestapo to gather evidence about "Röhm and his friendships," telling him, "this is the most important assignment you have ever received." Subsequently, Hitler had them all shot without trial. Röhm had been given the choice of committing suicide, but when he refused, he too was murdered. In a speech following the killings, Hitler told the German people that he had no regrets for having given "the order to cauterize down to the raw flesh the ulcers of this poisoning of the wells in our domestic life."[16]

Alan could not help being appalled by these murders in the name of a so-called normality that was still an open question for him. The walls of his room at Cambridge were decorated with pictures of young, male muscle-builders in swim trunks as well as of photos of Christopher. A teddy bear he called Porgy sat atop his bureau.

Although he had by now become physically involved with a member of his own sex, Alan did not yet consider himself a homosexual. The relationship was very different from the one with Christopher Morcom. The sexual aspect that had been lacking with Christopher was present, but the powerful emotional commitment was absent, at least for Alan.

The young man's name was James Atkins. Like Alan, he was a mathematical scholar at King's College, although not in Alan's league. At Alan's invitation, James went on a nine-day hike with him through England's Lake District. The third of those days was Alan's twenty-first birthday. A few days later, he and James had sex.

After they returned to Cambridge, James waited for Alan, who had made the first overture, to approach him again. When he didn't, James suggested they get together. Alan agreed, but qualified it with "If you want to go to bed, it'll be one-sided." Though confused about his sexuality, he was certain about his feelings toward James. There would never be any intense romance between them. They would be "satisfied with an easy-going sexual friendship in which there was no pretense of being in love."[17]

Nor, in the beginning, did their relationship prompt Alan to think of himself as gay. He was a very confused young man, and it was a very confused time where such matters were concerned. Not only were homosexual acts against the law, they were beyond the pale as far as most of society was concerned. Gay men were considered *queers* in the England of the 1930s. A student who startled Alan one day by snarling at him, "[Don't] look at me like that, I'm not a homosexual!" really shook him up.[18] Alan did not reply that he wasn't either; nor did he say that he was. No matter how

Alan felt, nor what he did, he simply wasn't sure what he was.

Alan didn't know that many young people, not just those who are gay, go through a period when they are confused about their sexual feelings. He thought it was just him.

It wasn't that he was in the closet so much as that he didn't really know what the closet was. He had loved Christopher, but there had never been anything physical between them. He had sex with James, but he felt no love for him. He knew he was different, eccentric even, but he didn't want to be queer. Alan just wanted to be himself.

If only he could be sure what *himself* was.

THE TURING 6 MACHINE

Historically, adults have always worried that the young are wasting their time with games when they should be developing the skills they will need in later life. Whether playing tag in the ancient Greek marketplace, or video games in the arcade, games have always been viewed by some as a distraction from more serious pursuits.

Yet games have played an important part in the advancement of mathematics. Euclid, whose theorems are the foundations of the geometry that students study today, was himself a game player. He set up puzzles having to do with points, lines, planes, and angles, and in solving them he created a whole new mathematics.

Early twentieth-century mathematicians related their theories to the game of chess and called it the *formalist approach*. David Hilbert was one of its leading advocates. Doing math, Hilbert believed, was like playing chess.

Born in Germany a half century before Alan Turing, he used the formalist approach to express mathematical theory for over thirty years. He viewed the axioms (mutually agreed-upon, self-evident truths) of mathematics as starting positions in a game of chess. He regarded the steps of a proof as chess moves. Definitions of what mathematics could do were like statements about the limits of chess—for instance, that a king alone cannot checkmate the other.

By 1930, when he was sixty-eight years old and had dominated the world of mathematics since the turn of the century, Hilbert had reached an important conclusion: "There is no such thing as an unsolvable problem."[1] Of course when he said that, Hilbert had never heard of the young Cambridge student Alan Turing.

Alan had played chess since childhood. As with the Japanese game go, which he also enjoyed, a large part of his feeling for chess stemmed from its mathematical structure. Like many others in the field, Alan related chess to mathematical theory and vice versa. Like them, he saw the similarities between working out a chess problem and working out a math problem.

At the same time, Alan was not a very good chess player. As he sometimes did in math and physics, he relied on intuition and challenged accepted wisdom with impulsive moves. He wanted to see how such moves played out more than he wanted to win the game. He would not agree to any theory of opening moves or strategy until he tested all possible variations, and there could be hundreds, even thousands of them. Alan was fond of chess for the same reason he was drawn to math: its logical organization. His shortcomings as a player were due to the same impatient nature that had disturbed his teachers. In math his mind too often jumped over the step-by-step proofs to the answer, and in chess the desired end result of a series of moves distracted Alan from the sequence itself. He was impatient with chess because he felt its theory didn't impact the real world. His teachers thought this lack of patience was his weakness as a student, but he would show that it could also be a strength.

To some extent, Alan had already proved it by June 19, 1934, when he graduated from Cambridge University "with distinction."[2] King's College awarded him a research grant of 200 pounds a year, which allowed him to stay on at Cambridge. But what he really wanted was a fellowship at King's. That would give him more security and more money than the grant.

By now he was focusing more on theoretical mathematics than on physics or the other sciences, and he had become interested in theories of probability and statistics. He zeroed in on a highly technical problem having to do with why scientific graphs (no matter what they deal with) tend to assume a specific pattern. What was the reason for this? Alan aimed to find out, to arrive at an exact answer, and to prove it by strict mathematical standards. This was the subject of the paper he submitted in applying for a fellowship at King's College. Alan called it the Central Limit Theorem.

Alan worked on the paper for a year, finishing it in the fall of 1934. Connecting pure mathematics with the physical world, it was typical both of his previous schoolwork and of the groundbreaking achievements that would follow. The Central Limit Theorem was the most original work he had done up to that time, and Alan had no hesitation in submitting it for the King's College fellowship.

It was brilliant. The fellowship judges all agreed on that. But there was a problem. Alan had neglected to delve deeply enough into the history of the problem he had tackled. The Central Limit Theorem had already been demonstrated twelve years earlier by another mathematician!

The previous proof was studied. The judges agreed that Alan's was superior, and they decided to accept it as a valid research paper. Soon after, they awarded Alan a three-year fellowship at 300 pounds a year. He would be a *don*—the title given in English universities to an instructor-tutor of undergraduates.

Only twenty-two years of age, Alan was very young for the post. Back at his old school, Sherborne, where his replica of Foucault's pendulum and other exploits had made him something of a legend, the boys celebrated his accomplishment with a double-edged verse:

Turing
Must have been alluring
To get made a don
So early on.[3]

A year later Alan entered his paper on the Central Limit Theorem in the Cambridge essay contest and won the Smith's Prize. The award was for thirty-one pounds. He had recently learned to sail and considered buying a boat with the money, but became busy with a new project and never got around to it.

His days of rowing with the Cambridge crew had ended with his graduation, and he missed being out on the water. He had, however, resumed running with a vengeance. Alan regularly ran marathon distances, and both his speed and endurance were improving remarkably. In the summer of 1935, while he was taking a break from one of these long runs in a meadow near a town called Granchester, his always active mind had a sudden insight into a question with which he had recently become obsessed.

The question was known as the *Entscheidungsproblem* (decision-making problem), which had been raised by David Hilbert. Is there, Hilbert wondered, an absolute method—a test—that can correctly determine whether any statement in mathematics is solvable? This was the Entscheidungsproblem.

Answering his own question, Hilbert concluded that the truth or falsity of a mathematical problem could always be determined. This could be accomplished by an "activity that could be performed by an automatic machine."[4] He didn't, however, say how, or what the activity would be, and he didn't define the machine.

In a Cambridge lecture on the "Foundations of Mathematics" attended by Alan, top-ranked mathematician M. H. A. "Max" Newman rephrased the Entscheidungsproblem. Could there be a mechanical process, Newman wondered, echoing Hilbert, that could determine if a mathematical assertion was provable? That phrase stuck in Alan's mind: *mechanical process!*

Lying in the meadow near Granchester that day and getting his second wind, Alan saw suddenly what it would mean to answer the Entscheidungsproblem by a mechanical process. The vague idea of a machine occurred to Alan. It was only an imaginary machine, of course, but the machine would be able to solve any question that was solvable.

Alan was beginning to deal with the Entscheidungsproblem in keeping with his nature. "Science, to Alan Turing," according to mathematician-biographer Andrew Hodges, "was thinking for himself, and seeing for himself, and not a collection of facts. Science was doubting the axioms."[5] Alan was not accepting the great Hilbert's proposition on faith; he was approaching it with skepticism.

He began with an old Greek paradox: A person says "I am lying." If that is so, then the speaker is telling the truth. But if the person is telling the truth, then he or she is lying. A lie, or the truth? Which is it?

Obviously, Turing realized, some questions simply cannot be solved. Surely this was as true of mathematics as of anything else. This, however, contradicted Hilbert's claim that "there is no such thing as an unsolvable problem."

At the same time, Turing recognized that there were solvable problems. Two plus two equals four; it is always possible to determine the answer to such equations. How then can we distinguish between problems that are solvable and those that are not?

Alan Turing at age six

Alan Turing at age sixteen

Euclid framed the axioms that govern geometry around 300 B.C. Instead of accepting the axioms on faith, Alan questioned them.

This woodcut shows Jean-Bernard-Léon Foucault
demonstrating his pendulum. As the audience
watched, the arc of the pendulum clearly began to
diverge from the line along which it originally swung.
The arc of the pendulum, however, had not changed.
In fact, the rotation of the earth had caused the floor
of the exhibition hall to move beneath the constant
swing of the pendulum. Alan built his own Foucault's
pendulum in the stairwell of his Sherborne dormitory.

David Hilbert: In answering Hilbert's question of whether all mathematical problems are decidable, Alan conceived the Universal Turing Machine.

The possibility of studying with the famous scientists Kurt Gödel (left) and Albert Einstein (right) drew Alan Turing to Princeton University. He also hoped to work with Alonso Church (not pictured).

◆ *The Allied shipping crisis made breaking the Enigma code the number-one priority of British Intelligence. Here, a German U-boat sinks a British vessel.*

▶ *The Enigma machine: Closest to the viewer is the plugboard. Above the plugboard is the keyboard and above that the screen on which the letters are illuminated. Above the screen are three dials that control the rotor positions, which can be seen through the small windows beside each dial.*

Bletchley Park

A decoded Enigma message: The German cipher clerks made the job of the British code breakers easier by routinely transmitting unnecessary messages such as, "nothing to report."

ADM
TO : I D 8 G   ZIP/ZTPG/33602
FROM : N S

5750 KC/S   T O I 0902/12/2/42
              T O O :- 1108

FROM : NAVAL D/F DETACHMENT, FLANDERS
          (M.P. ABT FLANDERN)

NO EVIDENCE OBSERVED HERE SO FAR IN WESTERN CHANNEL AND
DOVER AREA FOR DISCOVERY OF OUR OPERATION BY BRITISH
NAVAL AND AIR FORCES.

1040/14/2/42++++ EGT/BC+++

CORRECTION :- READ AS : FROM : NAVAL D/F DETACHMENT, FLANDERS

*Winston Churchill, prime minister of Britain,
thrived on the Ultra data.*

The Colossus machine

*Until his injury, Alan Turing hoped to
run in the Olympics.*

*Alan Turing (bottom left) in a photo of the
National Physical Laboratory (NPL) team*

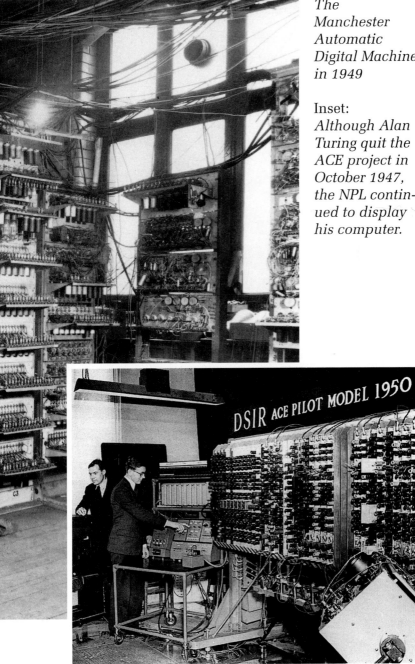

The Manchester Automatic Digital Machine in 1949

Inset: Although Alan Turing quit the ACE project in October 1947, the NPL continued to display his computer.

Alan Turing (right) at the console of another
Manchester computer in 1951

Alan Turing's work in artificial intelligence paved the way for later pioneers such as Raymond Kurzweil, pictured here in 1977. Kurzweil is still a leading force in the field of artificial intelligence.

Alan Turing's work also heralded the age of
virtual reality. Scientists at NASA's Johnson Space
Center are using this virtual reality system to
help train prospective astronauts.

Only by trying to solve them. This was Turing's premise. Put two pennies on the table and then put down two more pennies and you have four pennies every time. It is demonstrable. But try to determine if the statement "I am lying" is true or false, and a solution eludes you.

If this seems simple, remember that it wasn't quite so obvious to Hilbert and many other brilliant mathematicians. Only the step-by-step logic of mathematics itself was valid to them. So-called "common sense" was not a valid proof in mathematics.

Alan was caught between a rock and a hard place. He believed that the answer to the Entscheidungsproblem would be an action performed by a machine, a mechanical process, just as Hilbert had suggested. But the establishment was committed to *pure* mathematics. Its view was expressed by its most eminent spokesperson, G. H. Hardy, who had declared that "it is only the very unsophisticated outsider who imagines that mathematicians make discoveries by turning the handle of some miraculous machine."[6]

Perversely, from spring 1935 through April 1936, Alan focused on mechanical devices. In many ways, he was as much a tinkerer as he was a mathematician. He had seen the hundred-year-old model of the Analytical Engine designed by Charles Babbage in the London Science Museum. The calculating device had never been built, and might have been impractical because of its size, but the idea behind it was yet another link between the heady world of mathematics and the real world of machinery.

Babbage's Analytical Engine had been designed to eliminate much of the need for human action in performing mathematical functions. It would carry out a series of instructions on a punch card inserted into the machine. A remarkable woman mathematician who had worked with Babbage, the Countess of Lovelace, actually devised a program for the Analytical Engine. Today this is acknowledged by many computer scientists to be the world's first computer program.

Like the unbuilt Analytical Engine, Alan realized, a mechanical device that could illustrate mathematical undecidability would have to manipulate numbers. But numbers were only symbols, weren't they? Weren't they symbols just like the letters managed by a typewriter? You hit a typewriter key, and a letter appeared on the piece of paper inserted in the roller. If you held down the shift key on the typewriter while you struck the letter on the keyboard, you would type an uppercase, rather than a lowercase, letter. In response to the operator's actions, the typewriter was able to manipulate letters in a predictable way. Surely Alan could design a machine that could manipulate numbers. In some ways, Alan's theoretical machine resembled a typewriter, but in other ways it was very different. Although a typewriter was mechanical, each function it performed was separate and distinct and required a human being to trigger it. It was mechanical, but not automatic. Alan's machine would have to perform *automatically*. This meant it would have to perform its task without any human intervention. He designed such a machine. Alan called his machine a Turing machine. It was not really a specific machine but a class of machines containing an infinite variety of individual machines. Each one was remarkable.

A Turing machine consists of a head and a narrow paper tape that is divided into frames like those on a roll of film. The tape can be infinitely long—a benefit of an imaginary machine. Each frame may either be blank or printed with one symbol from a finite, prespecified set of symbols. The input tape, the tape as it is presented to the machine before it begins its task, may have a finite number of frames marked, or they can all be blank. At any step, the head can read the contents of a frame with its attached scanner. If the frame is blank, the head can either leave the frame blank or print one of the symbols. It can then move one frame to the right or left, or not move at all. If the frame already contains a symbol, the head can erase the symbol, replace it with a different symbol, or leave it alone. It can then move one frame to the right or left, or not move at all.

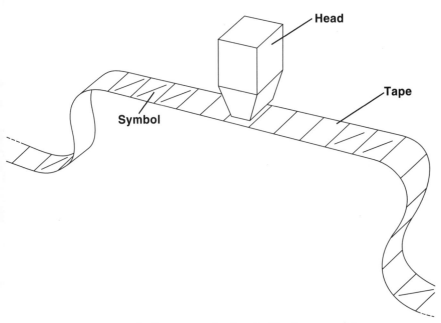

A diagram of a basic Turing machine

The head is programmed with a prespecified set of rules, or instructions. These instructions tell the head how to behave. As an example, imagine an instruction called INSTRUCTION A-1. This instruction is: if a * is scanned in the frame, erase the * and move one frame to the left.

There is more. Consider again an ordinary typewriter. In the initial configuration of a typewriter, when the "4" key is pressed, the machine prints a 4. When the operator holds down the shift key, the machine enters a new configuration. Now, pressing the "4" key results in the printing of a $. Turing named these configurations *states*, and like a typewriter, a Turing machine has multiple states. Unlike a typewriter, a Turing machine is automatic, so it cannot depend on an operator to press a key to cause the machine to change states. The state-changing command must be incorporated into the instructions. Therefore, for INSTRUCTION A-1 to be complete, it must be: if a * is scanned in the frame, erase the *, move one frame to the left, and enter state 5. State 5 is arbitrary in this example; an actual instruction would designate any state from a finite, prespecified number of states. Each state corresponds to a different set of instructions, so in state 5, the instruction upon reading a * may be completely different from INSTRUCTION A-1. The instruction sets for each state can be displayed in a table, called a rule table.

Consider this example of a very simple Turing machine that can do addition. It has a very small set of symbols—it can print only a / in each frame. The head is programmed with a rule table that will allow it to add together two separate strings of frames filled with / marks. In this example, the Turing machine will add a string of two / marks, representing the number 2, to a string of six / marks, representing the number 6. When it has finished its task, the Turing machine will produce at tape with eight consecutive / marks, representing the number 8.

This is the input tape:

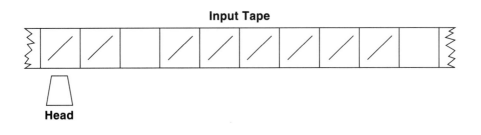

Input Tape

Head

The first string of slashes represents the number 2. The second represents the number 6.

This is the rule table:

STATE

SYMBOL SCANNED		1	2	3
	/	leave / move right state 1	leave / move right state 2	erase / no move state 3
	blank	print / move right state 2	leave blank move left state 3	halt

The instruction in the top left box tells the head what to do if a / is scanned in state 1. The instruction [leave / — move right — state 1] means, leave the / mark alone, move one space to the right, and remain in state 1. The instruction in the next box down tells the head what to do if a blank frame is scanned in state 1. The instruction [print / — move right — state 2] means, replace the blank with a /, move one space to the right, and go to state 2. Consequently, in state 1 the head will scan the / marks, leave them alone, and move to the right until it encounters the blank frame between the strings. It will then print a / in the frame, move right, and go to state 2. In state 2, the machine will continue to move to the right until the head encounters the blank space at the end of the second string. It will then move one space to the left and enter state 3. In state 3, the machine will erase the last / mark, not move, remain in state 3, and then halt, signaling the end of the task. The tape will then contain a continuous string of / marks, symbolizing the addition of the two initial strings.

Output Tape

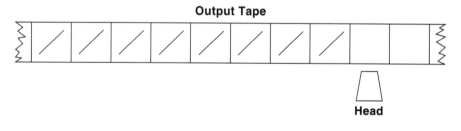

Head

The output tape

In this case, the string of two marks and the string of six marks have been added to create a string of eight marks. The machine has solved the problem 2+6=8, and it could similarly solve any simple addition of positive integers.

This is a very simple Turing machine with a very simple rule table. Turing, however, realized that a rule table could be created to solve any solvable problem. Some problems could not be solved by any rule table, but Turing knew that this was not a deficiency of the Turing machine. Hilbert was wrong. Some problems just could not be solved. There was no logical flaw in these problems, and unique answers could be shown to exist. Finding those answers with a mechanical process, however, was impossible.

An example of a problem that a Turing machine cannot solve, and cannot even determine if it is ultimately solvable, is the "halting problem." There exists, theoretically, a Turing machine that when started on a problem apparently will compute forever. It can't be proved, however, that it will compute forever. It also can't be proved that it will stop. Theoretically, it will do one or the other. There is an answer. It is just not solvable.

Alan had done it. He had designed a machine that disproved Hilbert. What his machine couldn't do was a milestone in mathematics. What it could do, however, was just as remarkable. He had designed an automatic problem-solving machine. No matter how many steps were involved, and no matter how complex the mathematical functions performed, once the process had been put in motion there would never be any need for human intervention until it was completed. Then the only human role would be to set the machine to another problem, or string of problems, for it could handle an infinite number, solving one after the other until it reached the end of the string.

At first he had thought of a class of machines containing an infinite number of specific machines. He discovered, however, that he could design machines with rule tables that could mimic the behavior of all other machines. These Turing machines encompassed all other conceivable Turing machines. Now, a single machine with a single rule table could solve all solvable problems. He called it a Universal Turing Machine.

Alan had conceived an imaginary machine with an infinite storehouse for information and instructions. His simple design demonstrated how such a machine would work. It would not just process mathematics; it could be programmed to process symbols representing values in virtually every field of human endeavor. Actually, Alan had designed a computer.

The tape was its memory bank. Both instructions and data could be stored on it. The rule table was its operating system, telling the head how to act on the data printed on the tape. Although the Universal Turing Machine has never been built, it is the forerunner of every computer in existence today, no matter how complex. The simple principles Alan Turing laid down for the processing of data and instructions are followed by all computers. The Universal Turing Machine is the standard by which all existing computers, and all computers to come, are defined.

Of course Alan's original aim had not been to design a computer. It had been to devise a mechanism that would answer the Entscheidungsproblem. It had been to disprove Hilbert's assertion that all mathematical problems were decidable. It had been to demonstrate that there is no absolute method—even with an automatic machine of unlimited capabilities—for determining whether every statement made in mathematics is provable. Alan's aim had been to prove, contrary to Hilbert, that there are such things in mathematics as unsolvable problems. The Universal Turing Machine had done that.

As Stan Augarten sums it up in his excellent book

on the history of computers, *Bit by Bit*, "Turing had come up with a litmus test of decidability—a mechanical method that showed that the only way to determine whether a statement was true or false was . . . to try to solve it." Augarten goes on to point out that "no machine, even a computer equipped with an infinite storehouse of information and instructions, can answer every problem; on the other hand, a machine with the slimmest of operational abilities can solve a phenomenal range of problems, and this was Turing's first great contribution to our understanding of computers."[7]

On May 28, 1936, Alan submitted his paper on the Universal Turing Machine entitled *On Computable Numbers with an application to the Entscheidungsproblem* to the London Mathematical Society for publication in its journal, *Proceedings*. A year earlier he had applied for a fellowship to Princeton University in the United States. Princeton was in the process of becoming a mecca for leading mathematicians and physicists from all over the world. The work being done there was on the cutting edge of mathematics, and Alan wanted to be a part of it.

He did not win the fellowship, but decided to go to Princeton anyway and pay his own expenses. On September 9 he paid a farewell visit to Christopher's mother. Mrs. Morcom recorded in her diary that Alan planned "to study under 2 great authorities on his subject" at Princeton, referring to Kurt Gödel and Alonso Church.[8]

On September 23, when Alan sailed for America, Alonso Church in particular was much on his mind. He had recently learned that the eminent mathematician Church had also published a paper demonstrating that Hilbert was wrong about the Entscheidungsproblem. Alan had not seen Church's paper, but he feared it would overshadow his own work.

And so it did at the time—but not in the long run.

THE WAR YEARS

During his two years at Princeton, there were times when Alan was so depressed he thought about killing himself. He wrote about these feelings in a letter to James Atkins. The suicide method he was considering involved hooking up an apple to electric wiring.

His affair with James, casual but long-lasting and as much a matter of friendship as passion, had been interrupted by Alan's departure, but would resume when he returned to England. Meanwhile, Alan had no outlet for his feelings, and there was no one with whom he could discuss them. As a gay foreigner, he felt much more alienated at Princeton than he had at Cambridge.

Princeton was as isolated from the rest of the United States as Cambridge was from Great Britain. Both countries were in the midst of the Depression, unemployment was extremely high, and food, clothing, and shelter were problems for great numbers of people. The two universities, however, were ivory towers standing well above those less fortunate while catering to a relatively well-off student body and an intellectual elite.

Alan was surely part of this elite, but he did not easily integrate into it. He was not openly gay, but he knew that he was different and recognized that others knew it too. In the Great Britain of the 1930s, harsh laws were enforced against homosexuality, but within the confines of Cambridge there had been some tolerance toward it. In the United States, such laws varied widely from state to state and frequently went unenforced. However, at Princeton Alan sensed a widespread attitude that homosexuality simply did not exist. It was not so much frowned upon as neither acknowledged nor discussed. A gay male at Cambridge might be ridiculed and humiliated. At Princeton he was simply ignored. Alan could stand abuse more easily than the rejection of being ignored.

One specific rejection came from a young American student named Venable Martin. Alan had helped him understand the mathematical logic in a course he was taking, and they had become friends. When they went canoeing together, Alan expressed an "interest in having a homosexual relation."[1] Martin's reaction made it clear that he wasn't gay. But he didn't reveal Alan's offer to anyone until years later and continued his friendship with Alan.

Despite his alienation, Alan's first impression of Princeton's academic program was positive. "The mathematics department here comes fully up to expectations," he wrote his mother. "There is a great number of the most distinguished mathematicians here."[2] He went on to mention Albert Einstein, G. H. Hardy, and Alonso Church, among others.

Naturally, Alan had mixed feelings about meeting Alonso Church. His own paper on the Entscheidungsproblem had not yet been published, but Church's work was known to the other mathematicians at Princeton and much admired. As for the Universal Turing Machine, Alan suspected—correctly, as it turned out—that it would not be of primary interest to mathematicians.

When he did meet Church, Alan wrote home that "I get on with him very well." But as far as working with Church was concerned, he added, "I don't know how much I shall have to do with this program of his, as I am developing the thing in a slightly different direction."[3] It was typical of Alan to remain a loner at Princeton and to diverge from the mainstream.

His hero Einstein, it seemed, was also a loner. Alan caught glimpses of him in the hallways, but had no direct contact with him. Even after copies of Alan's article describing the Universal Turing Machine—published in London in January 1937—reached Princeton, Einstein took no notice of him.

Reaction to the paper was generally lukewarm. It did not make much of a stir back in England, and as for Princeton, Alan wrote his mother, "I was disappointed by its reception here."[4] Alonso Church was the illustrious mathematician, and Alan was still only an exchange student.

The paper's audience vastly underestimated the importance of the Universal Turing Machine. Alan had answered one of the most important questions in mathematics. He had laid down the rules for a branch of science that did not yet exist. He had conceived of a decision-making machine—the computer—and drawn up plans to show how it would work. He established limitations that applied not only to his original design, but to all future models, no matter how they improved on the original. Many years later *The London Times* would recall that "the discovery which will give Turing a permanent place in mathematical logic was made not long after he had graduated [from Cambridge]."[5] And the writer P. N. "Nicholas" Furbank would point out, "It is now widely known that he [Alan Turing] was . . . the inventor of the computer."[6]

The unenthusiastic reception given "Computable Numbers," as Alan's paper on the Universal Turing Machine came to be known, deepened his depression. He dealt with it as he had been doing for years. He rode his bicycle long distances. He went rowing. And, most frequently, he ran.

Running was always more than a sport or a way of

keeping in shape to Alan. Increasingly, it was necessary to his mental health. At the same time, it began to dawn on him just how good at it he was becoming. Back at Sherborne he had been a failure at most games, and this had made him think of himself as physically hopeless. Running, more than anything else, changed that. Now he was running longer and longer distances, and when he clocked himself, he was covering them in shorter and shorter times. In the back of his mind there was a dream. He wanted someday to qualify for the Olympics.

The dream took Alan's mind off his disappointment over how little attention was being paid to his paper. There was one group, however, that was paying a great deal of attention to it. These were the British Intelligence officers who ran the top-secret Government Code and Cypher School. They recognized that the mind behind the Universal Turing Machine could build an important bridge between abstract mathematics and the real world of code breaking. They approached Alan even before he left for Princeton, and soon after his return to England on July 18, 1938, they contacted him again.

In addition to earning his Ph.D. at Princeton, Alan won a Procter Fellowship. It meant he could stay on at Princeton as assistant to John von Neumann, who was second perhaps only to Einstein in the world of physics and mathematics. But Alan decided to pass it up. He was homesick for Cambridge; his fellowship there had been renewed, and he decided to take it.

But the onrush of history changed his plans. Italy, having conquered Ethiopia, signed a security pact with Germany. Hitler's troops were welcomed into Austria and now threatened Czechoslovakia. For England, war was only a matter of time. Alan agreed to join the code breakers at Bletchley Park. He plunged into working with the Bombes to break the Enigma codes.

Although this required his utmost concentration,

Alan was not blind to what was happening in the world around him. When his sympathies were aroused by the plight of the Jewish refugees who had fled to England to escape Nazi persecution, Alan acted. "He took a real interest in his fellow creatures," his mother would recall. "Though he had no more than the salary of a Fellow," she wrote, "just before the Second World War he made himself responsible for all the expenses . . . of an Austrian refugee of fifteen . . . and later paid all his expenses at Manchester University."[7]

After England entered World War II at the beginning of September 1939, keeping up with Enigma messages required more and more low-level code breakers to perform the routine tasks associated with the Bombes. By summer of 1940, Alan found himself in charge of about one hundred underpaid and overworked young women. One of these was Joan Clarke, who had been a student of botany and mathematics before the war interrupted her education.

Those who worked with Alan had different opinions of him as a boss. One subordinate said that he "impressed us all with his championing of the underdog and his willingness to help others." And Dr. I. J. "Jack" Good, a young mathematician who played chess with Alan at Bletchley, recalled that he "had an impish sense of humor, some of which was directed at authority."[8] On the other hand, some of the young women complained that he was harsh and unfriendly and walked past them as if they weren't there.

One young woman that Alan did not ignore was Joan Clarke. He came to know her outside of the code-breaking room as a skillful chess player. At first they had only a small pocket set with cardboard pieces that strained their eyes and took some of the pleasure out of their games. But they got hold of some clay, sculpted a set of chessmen, and baked them on a coal stove. They played several times a week, usually following Joan's nine-hour stint as a cryptanalyst. Noting the effects of a full day's decoding on both of them, Alan called their games "sleepy chess."[9]

Joan was the daughter of a London clergyman. Because she had been to university and liked to read, some of her coworkers at Bletchley regarded her as a bluestocking (a bookish and intellectually snobbish woman). Some of the men referred to her as that "female mathematician."[10] Although she was laid back in her dealings with others, her brightness may have put them off, particularly the men. But it didn't alarm Alan.

Her quickness of mind attracted him, and he enjoyed talking to her. Joan seemed to enjoy their conversations too, and she wasn't irritated by Alan's stammer as some other people were. They began going to the movies together. They took long walks. They spent some weekends in each other's company.

Joan had studied botany, and a technique she passed along to Alan revived his interest in "watching the daisies grow."[11] They had taken a long bicycle ride together and were resting in a field before starting back when they drifted into a discussion of plants. Alan recalled the *Fibonacci numbers*, which related to their growth and form.

The Fibonacci numbers, as Joan knew, were a connecting point between botany and mathematics. They referred to the patterning of leaves, flowers, and other plant growths. This patterning followed a numerical progression in which each step was the total of the previous two steps. For instance:

1-1-2-3-5-8-13-21-34, etc.

Now Joan showed Alan the practical application of the Fibonacci numbers in plant study. She demonstrated how to follow the leaves on branches upwards and pointed out how the number of leaves and the number of spaces between them replicated the Fibonacci series. The same applied to the arrangement of flower petals. Finally Alan picked up a cone from a fir tree, and he and Joan traced a clear pattern of Fibonacci numbers.

For Alan this revived an interest in nature harking back to his boyhood experiments with seaweed. During the years that followed he would come back to the subject many times. In his final years, he would involve himself in it deeply.

Their mutual interest in mathematics and nature drew Alan and Joan closer and closer together. Soon coworkers at Bletchley were gossiping about them and guessing at a romance. Perhaps this generated a pressure to which Alan felt he must surrender. In any case, in the spring of 1941, Alan asked Joan to marry him and she accepted.

Why? Although Alan was in the closet, he had long since admitted to himself that he was attracted to men, not women. He was not bisexual. As much as he liked Joan, did he really want a wife?

"I do love you."[12] He spoke these words to her more than once. He meant them, but only in the way one friend speaks them to another friend regardless of gender. And there were other words he spoke to Joan shortly after they agreed to marry.

He blurted out to her, wanting to be honest, that he had "homosexual tendencies."[13] But he didn't tell her the whole truth. He didn't tell her that he had acted upon them. He didn't tell her that he had been a party to same-sex experiences. He didn't tell her about his relationship with James Atkins.

"Tendencies" were not enough to deter Joan. They visited each other's families, and they announced their engagement. Following the announcement, they spent just about all of their spare time together. One exception was a day-trip Alan took with a friend to dig up the silver bars he had buried. By now the German armies were fighting pitched battles in Russia and North Africa, and it was clear that the Germans would not invade England. British currency was not going to be devalued, so Alan decided to dig up his treasure and convert it back to English money.

The expedition—and another that followed at a later date—was a failure. Alan couldn't remember which bridge marked the spot where he had hidden the Benzedrine inhaler. The inhaler contained the coded directions to where the two silver bars were buried.

He gave up on the inhaler and searched for the bars without the directions. The terrain had changed with the passing seasons, so Alan used a metal detector he had designed specifically for the search. He zeroed in on a place where he thought he had buried one of the bars. But he had misremembered, and while he and his friend succeeded in digging up quite a few pieces of scrap metal, they found nothing that was worth anything. In trying to protect the value of his money, Alan had lost it all.

It was not in his nature to brood over the loss. Indeed, he and Joan laughed about it. Wealth was never Alan's first priority in life, and neither was it Joan's. They put the loss out of their minds and continued making marriage plans.

They talked about having children. Alan said he wanted them. So did Joan. This, after all, was what society expected of British men and women during those wartime years—marriage, parenthood, the good life, the so-called *normal* life. Alan wanted it desperately. Too desperately, for it was not the life he was meant to live.

In the end, he decided that he couldn't go through with it. Besides his own torment, it wouldn't be fair to Joan. He confessed to her that he had acted on his "homosexual tendencies," that he had always been more attracted to men than women, that this would probably always be the case. Yes, he loved her, but he was afraid that if he married her it would destroy that love. Groping to help Joan understand his fears, Alan quoted Oscar Wilde's poem, *The Ballad of Reading Gaol* to her:

Yet each man kills the thing he loves,
By each let this be heard,
Some do it with a bitter look,
Some with a flattering word.
The coward does it with a kiss,
The brave man with a sword!

THE TURING TEST

8

Joan remained at Bletchley after Alan broke their engagement. Characteristically, he dealt with this awkward situation by plunging into work. He devised ways to improve the Bombes. He went on a secret mission to Washington, making the dangerous crossing through submarine-infested waters. He updated American code breakers on techniques for reading Enigma messages to chart German U-boat movements. He returned to Bletchley to find the Germans had improved Enigma once again.

England's "*Official Secrets Act . . .* prevented discussion of his wartime work," wrote P. N. Furbank in his preface to the four-volume collection of Alan's writings published after his death.[1] Postwar secrecy surrounding Colossus may have had to do with "some Colossus computers [being] moved to northern Iran," where they were "used in code-breaking efforts" against the Russians, according to *Time* magazine correspondent Robert Slater.[2] Whatever their reasons for withholding recognition of Alan's wartime accomplishments, the government didn't hesitate to exploit his genius after the war ended.

Victory in Europe was declared on May 8, 1945, and by the following month Alan had signed on as a "Scientific Officer" with the National Physical Laboratory (NPL) at Teddington. His assignment was "to design a prototype 'universal machine' or 'computer.'"[3] He would write a report, completed later that year, called *Proposals for Development in the Mathematics Division of an Automatic Computing Engine (ACE)*.

In this report, Alan insisted that "the computer have a hardware system that would be as simple as possible." He believed that the computer would function best by "programming, rather than by complex electronic circuitry."[4]

During the early years of computers this advice was ignored, and hardware became more and more complicated. However, with the development of the PC (personal computer) for use by people lacking a technical background, this trend has been reversed. Consequently, modern computers are more user friendly. Once again, Alan was ahead of his time.

In another section of the *Proposals*, Alan brought up "the idea of modifying a stored program . . . by the selective overwriting of instructions in memory." In other words, he suggested a method by which the operating system of a computer might be altered without replacing any of the hardware. "This gives the machine the possibility of constructing its own orders," he wrote, adding that "this can be very powerful."[5]

Alan worked alone on the *Proposals* for ACE. During the conceptual stages, according to Dr. James H. Wilkinson, who later joined Alan in the venture, "everything associated with the project had been done by Turing himself. He was a man with an original and inventive mind."[6]

Early in 1946, the executive committee of the National Physical Laboratory (NPL), consisting of a small group of scientific Fellows from the Royal Society, met to consider building Alan's ACE computer. There was a good deal of opposition. Some argued that it wasn't practical. Others protested that it would be too costly. A few insisted that the design was flawed and that it wouldn't work. Finally, however, 10,000 pounds ($50,000) was provided to construct ACE.

The amount was far from enough, so Alan had to redesign both the computer and its key programs. Reluctantly, he did this, and in 1947 he assembled an expert staff including Wilkinson, and construction began on a small model of ACE. By October, however, Alan became convinced that the NPL was never going to fund a full-scale computer. He quit the ACE project in disgust.

Throughout his two years with the NPL at Teddington, Alan continued his running. He joined the local Walton Athletics Club, and although he was basically a long-distance runner, he won both a 1-mile (1.6-km) and a 0.5-mile (0.8-km) race, as well as a 3-mile (4.8-km) handicap race. He wrote to his mother, "The track season is over now, but of course the cross country season will be beginning almost at once. I think that will suit me rather better, though the dark evenings will mean that my weekday runs will be in the dark."[7]

Alan took running very seriously. According to his mother, "He kept a careful check on his weight and timing" and guarded against "forcing his pace unduly."[8] Once, when his watch was being fixed, he tied an alarm clock around his waist in order to keep track of his speed. When visiting his mother, he usually ran the 18 miles (29 km) to her house.

In August 1947, he came in fifth in the Amateur Athletic Association Marathon Championship despite having taken time out to deal with a muscle cramp. By now there was serious interest in him as a runner, and the sports sections of the newspapers were doing stories on him. One London daily referred to him as a "star distance runner" in an article on him titled "Electronic Athlete."[9] His speed established him as a serious contender for the Olympic trials, and he began training for them.

Then disaster struck. He tripped while running one day and fell, smashing his hip. A bone had been displaced, and the doctors were unable to repair the injury. Alan had to give up any hope of running in the Olympic marathons. He would go on running to keep in shape, but he would not seriously compete in races.

Alan was thirty-five years old now, a bachelor, and highly respected as both a mathematician and computer scientist. Since the break with Joan, he had faced the reality of his sexual orientation and accepted it. Acceptance from his peers, however, did not follow. Once, in casual conversation with some colleagues, he mentioned to them that he was gay. They reacted with shock and disgust. This was, of course, typical of the attitude of British (and American) society at that time.

James Atkins had come to visit him at Teddington in the summer of 1946. During the war, James had been a conscientious objector. He had been sent to prison, but was released after four months to serve with distinction with a Quaker ambulance unit. Although Alan liked James and admired the way he lived up to his convictions, the relationship between them was always more physical than romantically satisfying. Mostly, Alan kept himself too busy with work to think about sex.

After leaving the ACE project he returned to Cambridge briefly to teach and do research. In 1948, he transferred to Manchester University to work on the construction of the Manchester Automatic Digital Machine. While he was there, in June 1949, Alan made a statement in an interview with the *Times* of London that provoked such skepticism, he began work on a theory to prove its validity. "I do not see why it [the computer]," Alan said, "should not enter any one of the fields normally covered by the human intellect, and eventually compete on equal terms."[10]

He had long been intrigued by the idea of machine

intelligence. Between June 1949, when his statement predicting computer intelligence appeared in the *Times*, and the following year, Alan worked on a paper dealing with the issue. He also spoke on it, both in lecture halls and over the British Broadcasting Corporation. He predicted that "One day ladies will take their computers for walks in the park and tell each other 'My little computer said such a funny thing this morning!'"[11]

Finally, in October 1950, Alan's long article, "Computing Machinery and Intelligence" appeared in the philosophical journal, *Mind*. It would subsequently be reprinted in many anthologies under the title "Can a Machine Think?" In the article, Alan asserted that they would be able to do so. He predicted that by the turn of the century, "One will be able to speak of machines thinking without expecting to be contradicted."[12] Inevitably, many other computer experts strongly disagreed.

The debate over potential machine intelligence spawned a search for a precise definition of what was meant by intelligence. Alan noted that intelligence did not mean always being right. The most intelligent work in science and mathematics often begins with errors. "If a machine is expected to be infallible," Alan wrote, "it cannot also be intelligent."[13]

Alan and a number of other mathematicians and philosophers argued fiercely about the nature of intelligence. Unfortunately, instead of coming closer to an exact definition of intelligence, the discussion seemed to make the concept of intelligence even more elusive. Alan became frustrated with the debate, which he felt had become an impediment to actual research in the development of thinking machines. He proposed a test that bypassed the endless arguing.

Everyone agreed that humans are intelligent, so this became Alan's benchmark. He would propose a game in which a machine tries to trick a human interrogator into thinking that the machine is another human. This became the essence of Alan's biggest contribution to the field of *artificial intelligence*—the *Turing test.*

The article in which Alan proposed the test begins by describing a party pastime called the *imitation game.* It is played by three people: a man, a woman, and an interrogator who may be either a man or a woman. The interrogator is in one room; the man and woman are unseen in another. The man is designated A, the woman B. The interrogator asks questions of both to determine whether A or B is the man. The answers are typewritten and slid under the door to him. It is A's objective to fool the interrogator. B's aim is to help the interrogator find out that A is the man. However, either A or B may lie in answering the interrogator's questions. "What will happen," Alan asked, "when a machine takes the part of A in this game?"[14]

The question then becomes which is the machine and which is the human being? It might seem that many answers would instantly give A away as the machine. A computer, for example, would be much faster at arithmetic than any human could be. However, an intelligent machine could be programmed to give strategic incorrect answers as well as correct ones. "Can a Machine Think?" points out that if the roles are reversed and the human is trying to fool the interrogator, the person "would be given away at once by slowness and inaccuracy in arithmetic."[15] But a person playing the game would get better at it with experience and could do sums more quickly knowing that wrong answers would not necessarily give him or her away. So too, Alan thought, would a machine improve its advanced skills. As with today's advanced computer chess programs, it would never make the same mistake twice.

He then considered what kind of machine would be able to take part in the imitation game. He anticipated the objections of computer engineers citing the limitations of computers as they then existed. "We are not asking whether all digital computers would do well in the game, nor whether the computers at present available would do well," he pointed out, "but whether there are imaginable computers which would do well."[16]

There followed a technical discussion of the nature of digital computers, what those already in existence were capable of doing, and what those that would follow them would be able to do. Alan drew parallels between operations performed by these digital computers and tasks carried out by people. He concluded that a computer, with "adequate storage" and the necessary "speed of action," that was run by "an appropriate program" would do as well as a human being in the imitation game.[17] Indeed, he thought computers would play it so well that "an average interrogator will not have more than [a] 70 percent chance of making the right identification after five minutes of questioning."[18]

Typically, Alan thought that the only way to determine whether the problem of machine intelligence was solvable was to try to solve it. He believed that the age of artificial intelligence would definitively begin when engineers successfully developed a machine that was observed to be acting intelligently. No matter how this activity is achieved, if a machine can fool a human interrogator into thinking it is intelligent, it is. But Alan knew that the idea of a machine thinking would upset many different groups, and so he tried to answer their objections in advance.

His paper first considered "The Theological Objection," which holds that since "thinking is a function of man's immortal soul . . . no animal or machine can think." Alan argued that this "implies a serious restriction of the omnipotence of the Almighty" and His ability to confer a soul on a machine if He wished.[19] Alan took pains to make the point although he did not really expect religious believers to accept it.

He next addressed the "'Heads in the Sand' Objection" expressed by those who found "the consequences of machines thinking . . . too dreadful" to be true. He attributed this view to "intellectual people" who "base their belief in the superiority" of humanity on the individual's ability to think. With a sarcasm too often typical of him, Alan thought "consolation would be more appropriate" for those threatened by machine intelligence than any answer to their emotional arguments.[20]

More-substantial objections by mathematicians were not so easily dismissed. Even a computer with an infinite capacity, they insisted, would be limited by its programming. It could act only according to its input— the information fed to it by human beings in the first place. This was "a disability of machines to which the human intellect is not subject."[21]

Alan thought that eventually computers might be programmed so sophisticatedly that they could produce ideas beyond the scope of their initial programming. Besides, Alan noted that there was no proof that the human intellect was free of such limitations. In his biography, Andrew Hodges records that Alan believed "that even his own originality must somehow have been determined."[22] Why hold computers to standards that we don't measure up to ourselves?

Alan also considered creativity. In his paper, he quoted a 1949 speech by Sir Geoffrey Jefferson: "Not until a machine can write a sonnet . . . because of thoughts and emotions felt," Professor Jefferson had pointed out, "could we agree that machine equals brain."[23]

Discussing this section of Alan's article, Andrew Hodges makes the point that "if a machine could argue as apparently genuinely as a human being, then how could it be denied the existence of feelings that would normally be credited to a human?"[24] Alan himself did not deny that human emotions were unique and mysterious. "But," he observed, "I do not think these mysteries necessarily need to be solved before we can answer the question [of whether a machine can think]."[25] This was the point of the imitation game—if we can define intelligence in the form of a test, then the impossible task of isolating every component of intelligence can be avoided.

In conclusion, Alan considered the nature of what he called "learning machines" and what we call computers. The extent of their powers, he explained, would be dependent on programming. He saw the need for some advances in engineering, but it was the software that would enable the machine to think. The first attempts in developing intelligent machines would focus on very narrow, abstract subjects like chess, but he repeated his prediction that "machines will eventually compete with men in all purely intellectual fields."[26]

This prediction, like the whole of "Can a Machine Think?", was regarded as science fiction by many of his professional contemporaries. Some computer experts feared that if it were taken seriously by the public, the whole field of computer science would be viewed as dangerous and funding to develop it would dry up. Others simply thought he was off the wall. They viewed the Turing test—as the imitation game came to be called—as a parlor game.

To a very few, however, it blazed a trail that would lead to what we now know as artificial intelligence. With the invention and advance of microchips, computer operations can now be processed much faster, and many of the feats Alan anticipated are now being performed.

Still, artificial intelligence is as controversial today as it was in Turing's time. Much of the objection to it echoes the objections he argued against. You can build a machine to do things, but that doesn't mean it thinks; this argument is still widely made. But Turing's test still satisfies almost everyone. Many believe that it will never be passed, and to date, no computer is close. Some of the staunchest critics of artificial intelligence, however, acknowledge that if a machine can clearly and consistently pass the Turing test, then the critics will be silenced.

Perhaps the most interesting prophecy regarding the Turing test came from a man who opposed the very idea of machine intelligence. Debating Alan over the BBC on January 14, 1952, Sir Geoffrey Jefferson greeted his predictions of thinking machines with irony: "It would be fun some day Turing," he said, "to listen to a discussion . . . between two machines on why human beings think that they think."[27]

Alan nodded. That *would* be interesting. And he laughed his cackling, mad-scientist laugh.

"CRIME" AND PUNISHMENT

The English city of Manchester in the years following Word War II was an overcrowded metropolis of more than two and a half million people. Manchester University, home of the Institute of Science and Technology, was one of the largest universities in Britain, with an enrollment of about 15,000 students. Following publication of the controversial article that introduced the Turing test, Alan lectured at the University College. His innovative work had gained him a certain renown on campus, but despite newspaper interviews and radio debates, he was not very well known in Manchester beyond the university. This worked to his advantage in an area of the city where recognition might have damaged his reputation.

In England, as in the United States in those days, gay people migrated to urban centers like Manchester. Here they were not so visible as in rural villages with sparser populations and narrower moral codes. Here they could meet other gay people in environments where they could feel at ease. While most of Manchester was as prejudiced against gay people as the rest of England, there was at least one area where—except for the persecution of the occasional police sweep—they could relax and be themselves.

This area, known as Oxford Street, ran for about 1 mile (1.6 km) from a railway bridge to a movie theater.

Along this stretch was an amusement arcade, several fish-'n'-chips shops, and a few pubs. At one of these, the Union Tavern, Alan was an occasional visitor.

He went there infrequently because the area was tawdry. Prostitutes worked Oxford Street, and muggings were not uncommon. In this setting, the Union Tavern was an oasis, a gathering place for gay people where strict order was maintained so that the often homophobic police would have no excuse to raid it.

Alan lived in Wilmslow, a small town 10 miles (16 km) south of Manchester. The house was called Hollymeade, and Alan had bought it in the summer of 1950. Here he embarked on a new research project having to do with morphology, defined in *Merriam-Webster's Collegiate Dictionary (10th ed.)* as "a branch of biology that deals with the form and structure of animals and plants."

The subject might seem a far cry from his work on computers, but actually Alan's interest in biology had been revived while he was formulating the logic of the Turing test. To deal with the workings of a machine brain, he naturally had to consider the human brain. He could build a machine brain. Indeed, he had. But how did a living brain get to be a brain? The question led him to the study of *morphogenesis*—"evolution as applied to structural forms."

In typical Turing fashion, he didn't limit his inquiry to the brain but considered the more general question of how any living organism becomes what it is. This took him back to an earlier time in his life when his first scientific interests had been in biology and chemistry. He remembered the experiments of his youth: the fruit flies, the alkaloids, and the iodine from seaweed. Now he thought that by studying biochemistry—the chemistry of living tissues—he might uncover the patterning (in other words, the mathematical formula) by which "an assemblage of cells 'know[s]' that it must settle into a five-fold symmetry . . . to make a starfish."[1]

Remembering his days in the country with Joan Clarke, he zeroed in on the Fibonacci numbers as a key to the solution. "How could the Fibonacci pattern of a fir cone be imposed . . . upon the growing plant?"[2] How did a fertilized egg become a chicken? How did a spherically symmetrical mass of cells develop into "an animal, such as a horse, which is not spherically symmetrical?"[3] How did any living matter take shape?

Such questions led him inevitably into genetics, which involves mathematics as well as biochemistry. Alan "was asking how the information in the *genes* could be translated into action."[4] He addressed the problem in November 1951 with a treatise called *The Chemical Basis of Morphogenesis.*

The paper was intended by Alan to be only a first step pointing a direction for further research. The following summer it was published by the Royal Society. But by then Alan's involvement with a young man named Arnold Murray had yielded serious consequences.

Arnold Murray had been convicted of stealing and was on probation when Alan met him. He came from the Manchester slums, was nineteen years old, unemployed, and in need of money. Occasionally, Arnold exchanged sex for cash.

It was only later that Alan would find this out. He was drawn to Arnold by certain similarities to himself. Arnold was interested in science and had experimented with chemistry early in his teens. He had been picked on by other boys because of his "intelligence and sensitivity."[5] He was thin and appeared vulnerable—not unlike Alan at that age.

Alan had encountered Arnold on Oxford Street and took him to a restaurant there. He was attracted by Arnold's liveliness and quick humor. His shabbiness aroused Alan's sympathy. Alan gave Arnold his address in Wilmslow and invited him up for the weekend.

Although he'd said he would come, Arnold stood Alan up. When Alan, by chance, ran into him again, Arnold apologized with a weak excuse. Nevertheless, Alan issued a second invitation, and this time Arnold appeared.

There were other visits. During one of them, they talked about politics and science. If they were to have a relationship, Alan didn't want it to be just sex. "There's got to be more," Alan insisted. Arnold seemed also to want more. But he didn't always understand what Alan was saying and this frustrated Alan. "I've got to teach you," he insisted.[6]

Arnold spent the night. Over breakfast the next morning, Alan tried to give him some money. Arnold's need was obvious to him, and Alan made the offer gently. Nevertheless, Arnold refused the cash. After he left, however, Alan discovered that the money in his wallet had been taken. He wrote Arnold a letter, not mentioning the missing bills, but making it clear that he didn't want to see him again.

At this time, Alan was still working hard to develop his theories on morphology. His work on this subject would be posthumously published as a book, and in his introduction to it, the editor, P. T. Saunders, pointed out that Alan had seen "the development of an organism from egg to adult as being programmed in the genes and . . . set out to study the structure of the program."[7] In other words, Alan had detected a similarity between programming for computer functions and genetic actions.

Some of this material was presented by Alan in speeches to members of the Neurological Research Unit of the Medical Research Council in London. Saunders believes that it may have laid the groundwork for discovering the structure of *DNA* (the basic material in the *chromosomes* that transmits the hereditary pattern). Alan's mother believed that Alan's theory could be applied "to malignant growths and thus promote cancer research and open the way to the discovery of a cure."[8] Such DNA research is being pursued actively today.

Alan was breaking new ground, but there was a distraction. Despite his letter attempting to end the affair, one day Arnold turned up at his house. When the youth demanded to know why Alan had rejected him, Alan told him. Arnold denied taking the money and was extremely convincing. So much so that Alan not only believed him, but also lent him three pounds. On his next visit, Arnold borrowed another seven pounds from Alan.

Two days later, on the evening of January 23, 1952, Alan came home to find that his house had been broken into and robbed. Nothing of great value had been taken. He was missing pants and a shirt, some shoes, razors, knives, a compass, and a bottle of wine. Actually, he couldn't be quite sure what was gone, but he made it a total of fifty pounds for the insurance company. To collect the insurance, he had to report the burglary to the police.

He didn't tell them that he suspected Arnold. But he was furious, and he wrote to Arnold, accusing him of the theft. He demanded that Arnold return the money he had loaned him, and told him that if he came to the house again, he would be turned away.

But Arnold did come to the house, and Alan did let him in. Arnold swore he had nothing to do with the robbery, and when Alan was skeptical he threatened to make their relationship public. Then Arnold calmed down and blurted out that while he himself had nothing to do with the robbery, he thought he knew who was responsible.

Arnold told Alan about a friend named Harry, a petty thief who hung around Oxford Street. He said that he had told Harry about visiting Alan and what a nice house he had. Harry had responded by trying to get Arnold to join him in robbing Alan. But, Arnold insisted, he had refused to have any part of such a scheme.

Although Alan was not entirely convinced, he gave Arnold a drink and had one himself. Then they went upstairs to bed. In the middle of the night though, Alan got up and stole downstairs. He took the glass Arnold had drunk from and hid it to give to the police. They could check Arnold's fingerprints on the glass against those found on the door through which the robber had forced entry.

In the morning Alan went to the police station. He told the police about Arnold's friend Harry, making up a story to explain the source of the information. Alan's thinking was very confused. He was afraid that Arnold or Harry might blackmail him. But if fear of blackmail was the reason for shielding Arnold, then it was self-defeating. It aroused the very suspicion he was trying to avoid.

The police saw through his cover-up story. When they interrogated Harry, they pursued their suspicions. The thief, caught with some of Alan's property in his possession, was quick to try to cut a deal for leniency by blabbing everything he knew about the homosexual relationship between Alan and Arnold. The constables went to Hollymeade and confronted Alan.

Wilmslow, unlike Manchester, was a small enough place for Alan, who had been on the BBC many times, to be something of a celebrity there. Homosexual acts were against the law, and if Alan had engaged in them, then the constables had hooked a much bigger fish than a small-time burglar. They questioned him energetically, and Alan was unable, or unwilling, to hide the truth. He told them everything. Subsequently, the police obtained a warrant and confiscated his letters from Arnold.

A few days later they arrested Arnold. He confirmed that sex had taken place with Alan. One of Britain's foremost code breakers, the originator of the ACE, the Universal Turing Machine, and the Turing test, the founder of computer science, a genius who was laying the theoretical groundwork for future genetic research, was arrested and charged with "Gross Indecency."[9]

On February 27, Alan and Arnold were arraigned in court and a date was set for trial. Bail was set at fifty pounds. Alan paid it and was released. Arnold couldn't make bail and remained in jail. The local papers had a field day with the story, reporting as many lurid details of the pair's alleged "crime" as they could get away with printing.

Alan did not let the publicity interfere with his work. The day after his arrest he spoke in London to members of the Medical Research Council. He had some new theories regarding morphogenesis, and he wanted their reaction to them.

At Manchester University, many of his colleagues avoided Alan. But while some former friends cut him dead, others went out of their way to show him support. His brother, John, obtained legal help for him, but made no secret of his disapproval of homosexuality. Alan's mother simply refused to accept the truth.

Alan was brought to trial on March 31, 1952. The twelve counts of "Gross Indecency" against him were read. He pleaded guilty to all of them, as did Arnold. Before sentencing, the judge listened to statements for and against leniency.

Some of Alan's most eminent colleagues testified for him. One called him "one of the most profound and original mathematical minds of his generation."

Another described him as "a national asset." But the prosecutor accused Alan of being "unrepentant" and quoted things he had said to prove it.[10]

Indeed, Alan did not repent. He could not feel that he had done anything wrong. He had hurt nobody. His partner had been as willing as he was. He had broken the law, yes, but it was an unjust law.

Still, he did not regard himself as a martyr. He kept his perspective and even contemplated his situation with some humor. He wrote:

The day of the trial was by no means disagreeable. Whilst in custody with the other criminals I had a very agreeable sense of irresponsibility, rather like being back at school. The warders [guards] rather like prefects [school monitors]. I was also quite glad to see my accomplice again, though I didn't trust him an inch.[11]

The judge gave Alan a choice between a year in prison and a year's probation during which he would have to undergo medical treatment designed to "cure" his so-called "condition." Alan chose the probation and treatment. It was an unfortunate choice.

Organo-therapy, as the treatment was called, was also known as "chemical castration."[12] It involved taking large doses of the female hormone, estrogen, by mouth. It was supposed to reduce Alan's sex drive and—in some unclear way—ultimately redirect it from men to women. The treatment was new and the side effects relatively unexplored.

Initially, it would make him impotent. But, he was assured, this would be only temporary and potency would return after the therapy had been completed. "I hope they're right," a worried Alan wrote a friend in April 1952.[13]

At first, while he was being treated, Alan continued

investigating and writing on morphology. The body of unpublished work he produced during this period, along with the notes for his lectures, would be included in *Morphogenesis*, one of the four books of his writings published almost forty years after his death. It would ensure him a place among the pioneers of biology in addition to his position as the founder of computer science.

It was a difficult year. The treatment did make Alan impotent. He had very little sex drive at all. His breasts grew larger. There may have been other consequences.

Studies have shown "that estrogen may have a direct pharmacological effect on the central nervous system" and "that learning can be influenced" and "performance may be impaired" by the drug.[14] If Alan's focus and concentration had been damaged, then this might have caused depression and despair. Or, the treatment itself may have altered his mood in this direction. No one really knew what the longer-lasting—or even permanent—effects might be. Alan had always been good at hiding his feelings, and there was no way to know the psychological impact of the drugs on him.

During the last three months of the treatment, implants of estrogen were inserted into Alan's thigh. Alan was sure that this was done to ensure that he remain impotent well beyond the period of his probation. He removed the implants. At the end of April 1953, the treatment and his probation were over. Ten months later, on February 11, 1954, as if confronting a fate and a future he had already envisioned, Alan made out a new will.

At that time, Alan involved himself in what he whimsically called "the desert island game."[15] The idea was to see how many common household substances he could make at home from scratch, using only raw materials. Among the materials he made, using large amounts of sodium hypochlorite, were a nonpoisonous weedkiller and a sink cleaner.

He also set about gold-plating an egg spoon. He melted down the gold from an old pocket watch that had belonged to his grandfather. He used coke (a form of coal that burns with intense heat) as an electrode, and he used potassium cyanide to facilitate the melting of the metal. He had long kept a jar of cyanide in a drawer for use in his lab work.

On Tuesday, June 8, 1954, late in the afternoon, his housekeeper discovered Alan lying in his bed. In the laboratory next to his bedroom, the gold plating apparatus was simmering. On the nightstand beside Alan's bed was a half-eaten apple. There was congealed white froth at the corners of his mouth. He had been dead for some time.

A medical examination revealed that he had died on June 7 of cyanide poisoning. The inquest that followed found that "the poison was self-administered while the balance of his mind was disturbed."[16] Alan Turing had committed suicide.

10 THE LEGACY OF ALAN TURING

In 1966, twelve years after Alan Turing's death, the Association for Computing Machinery (ACM), the major organization in the field of computer science, established the Turing Award. Presented annually, it is today regarded throughout the profession as "the Nobel Prize of computer science."[1] The first winner of the award was Alan J. Perlis, who paid homage to Turing by pointing out how his work had "captured the imagination and mobilized the thoughts of a generation of scientists."[2]

Some of these scientists, while working for the U.S. Defense Department at Yale University in the late 1970s, developed a computer research program and named it *CYRUS* after Cyrus Vance, who was then secretary of state. CYRUS was designed to cross-index and cross-reference newspaper articles about Secretary Vance on a daily basis. Before long the CYRUS databank held a considerable amount of information.

CYRUS, however, was intended to be more than just a databank. Its creators wanted CYRUS to *understand* the information, relate its various parts to each other and draw conclusions based on the raw material it had been fed.

To demonstrate its capabilities, CYRUS was asked what the chances were that the wife of the secretary of state had met the wife of Anwar Sadat, the president of

Egypt. There was no such meeting mentioned in the input data that CYRUS had been fed. CYRUS had to deduce the probability of such a meeting from facts indirectly related to the question.

To do this, CYRUS had to frame and answer a series of questions. Was Secretary Vance married? Was President Sadat married? Had there been a meeting between the secretary and the president? Was there more than one meeting? How many? How often did his wife go along with Vance on visits to heads of state? Did Mrs. Sadat customarily attend diplomatic functions? Etc.

Working its way through the questions and answers, CYRUS finally concluded that there was a 65 percent chance that the wives had met. CYRUS had studied and inter-related and evaluated the facts in its databank and then made an estimate, just as a person might. Some would argue that it had demonstrated an ability to reason.

CYRUS was an early example of what computer scientists today call artificial intelligence. Ten years after the Yale experiment, in the late 1980s, artificial intelligence had advanced into another area that Turing had anticipated: *artificial life.*

Turing had inferred similarities between the human brain and a machine brain, and this had led him to morphogenesis. He believed "that the solution" to the question of how forms evolved "was to be found in physics and chemistry." He tackled the problem with "the tools that he judged appropriate to the task, rather than those which . . . others were already using."[3] His innovative approach to the development of cells into forms, and to evolution, revealed new fields of inquiry to researchers in many disciplines, including biology, physics, mathematics, and computer science.

His genius laid the groundwork for the development of computer learning programs that could interact and spin off new programs in a lifelike fashion. Today the Santa Fe Institute, a research facility in Santa Fe, New Mexico, is dedicated to the study of artificial life.

He changed the world in which we live in other ways as well. Turing's work is an important part of the foundation on which computer programming innovator Jaron Lanier built *virtual reality*, the artificial sensory environment that a human being can inhabit. Within this remarkable environment, a person can explore and interact with an unlimited variety of things.

Today, NASA uses virtual reality to investigate space without leaving earth. Surgeons practice operations on imaginary patients. Children not only inhabit the world of dinosaurs, they become the dinosaurs in that world, experience the size, the awkwardness, the dangers. There is incredible potential to the uses of virtual reality. Turing's work has also influenced Raymond Kurzweil, the inventor of *Kurzweil Applied Intelligence* (KAI). Known as the smart machines, Kurzweil's creations are prime examples of the practical application of artificial intelligence. One of them allows a person and a voice-activated computer to communicate by using a 50,000-word vocabulary that the computer has been programmed to recognize. The program adapts as it goes along, making changes according to the instructions it receives, and learning from experience. It may confuse *to* and *too* and *two* the first time around, but subsequent reactions will be influenced by context.

One such program, operating with lightning speed, processes symptoms spoken aloud by a doctor as he or she examines a patient, and then indicates a diagnosis. The doctor's follow-up questions teach it to recognize paired symptoms and then combinations of symptoms, thereby refining and speeding up its diagnostic capabilities. Other Kurzweil machines scan books and read them to the blind, translate spoken words into print for the deaf, and interpret the garbled speech of cerebral palsy sufferers.

The world has become a very different place for everyone since the days of Alan Turing. Personal computers are common items in the homes, schools, and offices of America. The *Internet* has changed the world even more, and people all over the globe are able to get to know and understand one another. In some ways, the future anticipated by Turing is here, but in other, nontechnical areas progress has been slower.

Tolerance toward gay people is one such area. There has been some progress, but it has been hard to come by, and too often grudging. It is difficult to change attitudes and prejudices that have been passed down for generations.

"In 1952," as reported in Stephan Likosky's excellent anthology, *Coming Out*, "*Sunday Pictorial* [a British journal] published a series of articles on adult homosexuality called *Evil Men*."[4] While the articles were running, Alan Turing was being tried for gross indecency and a debate was raging in Britain over how to deal with gay people. On one side were those who stood by the laws that defined male and female homosexuality as both immoral and criminal. On the other were social scientists and doctors—psychiatrists and psychoanalysts mostly—who held that "the overriding consideration in dealing with homosexual offenders should be that it is a form of mental illness."[5] Gay people in Great Britain were trapped between being punished as lawbreakers and treated for some sort of ill-defined disease. Often, as in Alan Turing's case, the treatment was more damaging than the punishment.

The medical view was similar in the United States at that time. Among American establishment doctors, sex hormones were thought to be the principle factors in controlling masculinity and femininity. Treating male homosexuals with male hormones, however, proved no more effective than Alan Turing's treatment with female hormones. Anyway, gay men in the United States were much more likely to be locked up than treated.

Laws in both the United States and Britain reflected widespread antigay attitudes. In Britain "between 1931 and 1951 there had been a five-fold increase in prosecutions" of gay males.[6] The United States, in 1950, had "eleven states which allowed for compulsory castration [of gay men], with fifty thousand cases on record."[7] And at the time of Alan's conviction, U.S. federal law barred him from entering the United States because he had "a criminal record of moral turpitude."[8]

Change in the status of gay men and lesbians in America dates from June 27, 1969. On that Friday night, police raided the Stonewall Inn, a gay bar in New York City's Greenwich Village. Such raids of places where gay people congregated were routine police actions at that time, but this night was different. This night the gay patrons fought back. Bottles were thrown and the Stonewall was set on fire with the raiding police inside it.

The police were rescued, but the resistance was just beginning. There was a general uprising of angry gay people in Greenwich Village. It continued throughout the weekend, and by the time it was over, the Gay Liberation Front had been formed in New York City. Also, as historians John D'Emilio and Estelle B. Freedman point out, "The gay liberation impulse took root across the country, spawning scores of similar groups."[9]

They go on to discuss the changes that took place in the wake of Stonewall:

[During] the 1970s, half the states eliminated [antihomosexual] statutes from the penal code. In 1974, the American Psychiatric Association removed homosexuality from its list of mental disorders, and the following year the U.S. Civil Service Commission lifted its ban on the employment of gay men and lesbians. Several dozen cities . . . incorporated sexual preference into their municipal civil rights laws. . . . the national Democratic Party, at its 1980 convention, for the first time included a gay rights plank in its platform. . . . In most large cities, police harassment, though not eliminated, declined sharply. . . . Equality had not been achieved. Indeed, by the late 1970s a vocal, well-organized resistance to gay liberation had emerged. . . . But the gay movement had set in motion profound changes.[10]

"The case of Alan Turing dramatically illustrates the revolutionary change in thinking," according to Margaret Cruikshank, editor of *The Lesbian Path*, a journal for gay women. Discussing the treatment he was forced to undergo, she remarks that "this savagery has a tinge of medieval torture to it." She notes that such treatment would be unthinkable today, but finds that "the attitudes held by Turing's tormentors have not disappeared." Ms. Cruikshank notes a growing backlash that makes it particularly difficult for young gay men and lesbians to gain acceptance. She deplores the fact that "most middle-school and high-school students who are gay have no gay counseling programs at their schools."[11]

Signs of this antigay backlash are easy to find. Local school boards have banned books tolerant of "the gay lifestyle" from school libraries, rarely troubling to define what "the gay lifestyle" is. The "Don't ask, don't tell" rule preventing gay members of the military from identifying themselves has been imposed. Some politicians at all levels of government have openly declared their hostility toward gay men and lesbians.

Progress concerning gay rights has been a matter of two steps forward and one step back. Prominent people in a variety of fields have come out of the closet. These publicly gay figures include congressmen, state legislators, and city council members. There are people in government, both gay and straight, who use their power to fight for gay rights.

In England also, it has been a case of progress and backlash. To some extent, antihomosexual laws were eased by the Sexual Offenses Act in 1967. Laws "forbidding private homosexual acts between consenting adults" were repealed.[12] Inspired by Stonewall, gay liberation groups sprang up across England in 1969. One of the most militant was—and is—the London Gay Liberation Front. The group actively opposed Clause 28, an antigay measure designed to stop British schools from teaching "the acceptability of homosexuality."[13] Although the measure passed, the fight against its enforcement continues.

English lesbians and gay men are particularly angered by Clause 28 because it keeps them estranged from the larger society. It promotes the very sort of intolerance that crushed Alan Turing. It perpetuates myths of who and what gay people are, ensuring that another generation will grow to adulthood with the same antigay attitudes. It prevents the lesson of Alan Turing from being learned.

Alan Turing was eccentric. He was a genius, too. He failed at team sports but excelled at running. He was sometimes alienated and sometimes softhearted. He knew depression and he knew exultation, not because he was gay, but because he was human. His sexual preference was a part of him, but it did not define him.

Perhaps the lesson of Alan Turing is best embodied in *Outwitted*, an old Edwin Markham poem he learned while a student at Sherborne:

He drew a circle that shut me out—
Heretic, rebel, a thing to flout.
But Love and I had the wit to win:
We drew a circle that took him in.

Alan Turing drew a circle that took in a future generation that would live with the most advanced computer technology. They would reap the benefits of artificial intelligence and artificial life, of virtual reality and the Internet, and more. Alan Turing's circle takes in a bright new world—and myriad unknown worlds to come.

GLOSSARY

Alkaloids—organic compounds found in plants that combine with acids to form salts.

Artificial intelligence—the development of computers and computer programs that attempt to learn and reason.

Artificial life—a computer program that simulates the evolution of traditional life forms.

Automatic Computing Engine (ACE)—a prototype computer financed by the British government and designed by Alan Turing.

Blitzkrieg—a sudden overwhelming military attack.

Bombes—decoding devices used first by the Poles and later by the British to decipher *Enigma* messages.

Chromosomes—structures in the cells of all living things that contain *DNA* and *genes*.

Colossus—a decoding machine developed by the code breakers at Bletchley Park; one of the first operational electronic digital computers.

Cryptanalyst—a person who specializes in solving codes, such as the *Enigma code*.

CYRUS—a computer learning program named after former U.S. secretary of state Cyrus Vance.

DNA—an essential component of all living matter; the basic material in the chromosomes that passes on hereditary traits.

Don—an instructor-tutor appointed by an English university.

Enigma code—a code selected randomly by the *Enigma machine.*

Enigma machine—a device used by the Germans in Word War II to encode messages.

Entscheidungsproblem—a famous question in mathematics posed by David Hilbert: are all problems decidable?

Estrogen—the female hormone; also a chemical substance once used to decrease the male sex drive.

Euclid's axioms—a set of agreed-upon rules on which geometry is based.

Fibonacci numbers—a mathematical sequence that can be observed in patterns on plants.

Formalist approach—a mathematical discipline based on a formal system of rules.

Foucault pendulum—a pendulum that demonstrates the rotation of the earth.

Führer—the German word for "leader"; the title by which Hitler was addressed.

Genes—the segments of DNA containing hereditary data.

Genetics—the branch of biology concerned with hereditary traits.

Imitation game—a game in which an interrogator tries to distinguish between an unseen man and woman by their printed answers to questions; the basis for the *Turing test.*

Internet—a worldwide computer network.

Kurzweil Applied Intelligence (KAI)—the "smart machines" created by Raymond Kurzweil to compensate for such disabilities as blindness, deafness, etc.

Morphogenesis—the evolution of clustering cells into shapes.

Organo-therapy—also known as "chemical castration"; a medical procedure that treated homosexuality with large doses of *estrogen.*

Scanner—any mechanical reading device.

Turing test—a game proposed by Alan Turing to demonstrate the capability of a machine (computer) to think.

U-boat—a German submarine.

Ultra—the code name for decoded *Enigma* information; also used to refer to the entire secret British decoding operation.

Universal Turing Machine—an imaginary computer establishing a design and limits for all computers.

Virtual reality—an artificial sensory environment.

SOURCE NOTES

Chapter One
1. Phillip Knightley, *The Second Oldest Profession* (New York: Norton, 1987), 171.
2. John C. Nash, "The Birth of a Computer," *BYTE*, February 1985), 177.
3. Author's interview with computer expert Peter Brooks of Columbia University Teachers College.
4. Andrew Hodges, *Alan Turing, the Enigma* (New York: Simon and Schuster, 1983), 125.
5. Ibid., 124.
6. Knightley, 160.
7. Hodges, 205.
8. F. H. Hinsley, *British Intelligence in the Second World War, Vol. 2* (London: HMSO, 1981), 655.
9. Ibid., 657.
10. Knightley, 156.

Chapter Two
1. Hodges, 4.
2. Ibid., 6.
3. Sara Turing, *Alan M. Turing* (Cambridge, England: W. Heffer & Sons, 1959), 11.
4. Hodges, 6.
5. John Turing, *The Half Was Not Told Me* (unpublished autobiography), quoted in Hodges, 9.
6. Hodges, 7.
7. S. Turing, 12.

8. Hodges, 7.
9. S. Turing, 12.
10. Ibid., 17.
11. Ibid., 18.
12. Hodges, 11.
13. Ibid., 12.
14. P. T. Saunders, ed., *Morphogenesis: Collected Works of A. M. Turing* (New York: Elsevier, 1992), Preface, IX.
15. Hodges, 14.
16. Ibid., 17.
17. Ibid., 17–18.
18. S. Turing, 23.
19. Ibid., 22.
20. Ibid., 23.
21. Hodges, 21.

Chapter Three
1. S. Turing, 39.
2. Hodges, 22–23.
3. Nowell Charles Smith, *Members of One Another* (London: Chapman & Hall, 1913).
4. S. Turing, 27.
5. Hodges, 24.
6. Ibid., 30.
7. Ibid., 25.
8. Ibid.
9. S. Turing, 28.
10. Letter from D. B. Neild to Andrew Hodges, December 23, 1978.
11. Hodges, 29.
12. Ibid., 29–30.
13. S. Turing, 29–30.
14. Hodges, 29.
15. Ibid., 33.
16. Ibid.
17. Ronald W. Clark, *Einstein: The Life and Times* (New York: World Publishing, 1971), 73.

18. Hodges, 33.
19. Ibid., 34.
20. Ibid., 28–29.

Chapter Four
1. S. Turing, 36.
2. Hodges, 37.
3. S. Turing, 40.
4. Hodges, 57.
5. Ibid., 36–37.
6. Ibid., 36.
7. Ibid., 44–45.
8. Ibid., 40.
9. Ibid., 41.
10. Ibid., 38.
11. Ibid., 44.
12. Ibid.

Chapter Five
1. S. Turing, 36.
2. Ibid., 37.
3. Hodges, 52.
4. S. Turing, 37.
5. Ibid., 36.
6. Hodges, 52.
7. Ibid.
8. Ibid.
9. Letter from Patrick Barnes to Andrew Hodges, December 2, 1979.
10. S. Turing, 41.
11. Ibid., 38.
12. Hodges, 70.
13. S. Turing, 41.
14. Hodges, 71.
15. Ibid., 87–89.
16. Alan Bullock, *Hitler and Stalin* (New York: Alfred A. Knopf, 1992), 340–343.

17. Hodges, 76.
18. Ibid.

Chapter Six
1. C. Reid, *Hilbert* (London: George Allen & Unwin; Springer-Verlag, 1970), 113.
2. D. C. Ince, ed., *Mechanical Intelligence: Collected Works of A. M. Turing* (New York: Elsevier, 1992), VIII.
3. Hodges, 94.
4. Robert Slater, *Portraits in Silicon* (Cambridge, MA: MIT Press, 1987), 15.
5. Hodges, 79.
6. Ibid., 94.
7. Stan Augarten, *Bit By Bit: An Illustrated History of Computers* (Boston: Unwin Paperbacks, 1985), 144.
8. Hodges, 115.

Chapter Seven
1. Letter to Andrew Hodges from Dr. A. V. Martin, January 26, 1978.
2. Hodges, 117.
3. Ibid., 119.
4. Ibid., 124.
5. *London Times* Obituary Page, June 16, 1954.
6. Preface by P. N. Furbank, in Ince, VII.
7. S. Turing, 57.
8. Ibid., 71, 73.
9. Hodges, 207.
10. Ibid., 210.
11. Ibid., 208.
12. Ibid., 216.
13. Ibid., 206.

Chapter Eight
1. Preface by P. N. Furbank, in Ince, VII.
2. Slater, 17–18.
3. Ince, Introduction, VIII–IX.

4. Ibid., X.
5. Hodges, 324.
6. *BYTE*, February 1985, 177.
7. Hodges, 345–346.
8. S. Turing, 113.
9. *London Evening News*, December 23, 1946, Sports Section.
10. S. Turing, 91.
11. Ibid., 418.
12. Hodges, 417.
13. Ibid., 361.
14. A. M. Turing, "Can a Machine Think?", in James R. Newman, ed., *World of Mathematics,* (Redmond, WA: Tempus Books, 1988), 2076–2077.
15. Ibid.
16. Ibid., 2078
17. Ibid., 2082.
18. Hodges, 417.
19. A. M. Turing, 2083.
20. Ibid., 2084.
21. Ibid., 2085.
22. Hodges, 417.
23. A. M. Turing, 2083
24. Hodges, 423.
25. A. M. Turing, 2086.
26. Ibid., 2094, 2097.
27. S. Turing, 95.

Chapter Nine
1. Hodges, 430.
2. Ibid.
3. S. Turing, 105.
4. Hodges, 431.
5. Ibid., 449
6. Ibid., 453.
7. Saunders, Preface, XI.
8. S. Turing, 106.
9. Hodges, 458.

10. Ibid., 471–472.
11. Letter from A. M. Turing to Philip Hall, April 17, 1952.
12. Hodges, 471.
13. Ibid., 473.
14. D. E. Sands, "Further Studies on Endocrine Treatment in Adolescence and Early Adult Life" in *Journal of Mental Science*, January 1954.
15. S. Turing, 116.
16. Ibid., 117.

Chapter Ten
1. Author's interview with computer expert Peter Brooks of Columbia University Teachers College.
2. *ACM Turing Award Lectures Book: The First Twenty Years* (Reading, MA: ACM Press [Addison-Wesley], 1987), Preface, XVII.
3. Saunders, Preface, XI.
4. Stephan Likosky, ed., *Coming Out: An Anthology of International Gay and Lesbian Writing* (New York: Pantheon Books, 1992), 429.
5. G. Westwood, *Society and the Homosexual* (London: Gollancz, 1952), 166.
6. Hodges, 462.
7. A. Karlen, *Sexuality and Homosexuality* (London: Macdonald, 1971), 334.
8. Hodges, 474.
9. John D'Emilio and Estelle B. Freedman, *Intimate Matters: A History of Sexuality in America* (New York: Harper & Row, 1988), 319.
10. Ibid., 324.
11. Margaret Cruikshank, *The Gay and Lesbian Liberation Movement* (New York: Routledge, 1992), 56.
12. Leigh W. Rutledge, *The Gay Decades: From Stonewall to the Present; The People and Events That Shaped Gay Lives* (New York: Plume [Penguin Books], 1992), 8.
13. Cruikshank, 77.

FURTHER READING

By and about Alan Turing:

Hodges, Andrew. *Alan Turing, the Enigma.* New York: Simon and Schuster, 1983.
A comprehensive biography detailing Alan Turing's accomplishments in computer science, mathematics, and biology and covering his childhood and subsequent years as a gay male in England from the 1930s through the 1950s.

Ince, D. C., ed. *Mechanical Intelligence: Collected Works of A. M. Turing.* New York: Elsevier, 1992.
This collection of papers on computer science written by Alan Turing is recommended for high school students with a background in computers and an interest in artificial intelligence.

Saunders, P. T., ed. *Morphogenesis: Collected Works of A. M. Turing.* New York: Elsevier, 1992.
Alan Turing's papers on the mathematics of plant and animal growth and evolution are recommended for students and others interested in biology.

Turing, A. M. "Can a Machine Think?" in Newman, James R., ed. *World of Mathematics,* Redmond, WA: Tempus Books, 1988.

Most of the articles in this collection are easy to read, including Alan Turing's essay establishing the field of artificial intelligence; an excellent introduction to mathematics and computer science.

Whitemore, Hugh. *Breaking the Code.* Oxfordshire, England: Oxford Press, 1987.
An award-winning dramatic play based on Alan Turing's wartime code-breaking service and the events leading up to his suicide.

About Computers and Computer Scientists

Augarten, Stan. *Bit by Bit: An Illustrated History of Computers.* Boston, Unwin Paperbacks, 1985.
An easy-to-follow account of how computers developed (starting with the abacus) and how they work. The graphics are very helpful.

Baum, Joan. *The Calculating Passion of Ada Byron.* Hamden, CT: Archon Books, 1986.
A biography of the nineteenth-century British countess who wrote the first computer program.

Bernstein, Jeremy. *The Analytical Engine: Computers Past, Present and Future.* New York: Morrow, 1981.
A history of the computer, including information on Alan Turing.

Curran, Susan, and Ray Curnow. *Overcoming Computer Illiteracy: A Friendly Introduction to Computers: How They Work and What They Can Do for You.* New York: Penguin Books, 1984.
Just what the subtitle says; recommended for those who are computer-shy but would like to learn.

Haugeland, John. *Artificial Intelligence: The Very Idea.* Cambridge, MA: MIT Press, 1985.
An excellent survey of the history of artificial intelligence. Includes information on Alan Turing.

Kurzweil, Raymond. *The Age of Intelligent Machines.* Cambridge, MA: MIT Press, 1990.
A comprehensive guide to the history of computers and artificial intelligence written by a pioneer in the field. Includes information on Alan Turing.

Slater, Robert. *Portraits in Silicon.* Cambridge, MA: MIT Press, 1987.
Fascinating dramatic portraits of the men and women who developed computer science; includes a well-rounded chapter on Alan Turing.

World War II Code Breakers & Codes

Garlinski, Josef. *The Enigma War: The Inside Story of the German Enigma Codes and How the Allies Broke Them.* New York: Scribner, 1979.
Includes a detailed account of the Polish contribution to the Allied effort to break the Enigma code.

Kahn, David. *Seizing the Enigma: The Race to Break the German U-boat Codes, 1939–1943.* Boston: Houghton Mifflin, 1991.
The most recent and complete account of the effort to break the Enigma code.

Knightley, Phillip. *The Second Oldest Profession.* New York: Norton, 1987.
Intelligence and counterintelligence, their effectiveness and ineffectiveness in World War II and beyond.

Lewin, Ronald. *Ultra Goes to War: The Secret Story.* London: Book Club Associates, 1978.
How the data gathered by the Turing decoders was used to strike at the Nazis in World War II.

Winterbotham, F. W. *The Ultra Secret.* London: Weidenfeld & Bocolson, 1974.
The story behind the secrecy obscuring Alan Turing and the Colossus.

The Gay Civil Rights Struggle

Cruikshank, Margaret. *The Gay and Lesbian Liberation Movement.* New York: Routledge, 1992.
A serious discussion of how the movement developed and what it means to be a gay man or woman in America today.

Fletcher, Lynne Yamaguchi. *The First Gay Pope and Other Records.* Boston: Alyson, 1992.
A survey of prominent gay men and women in history.

Rutledge, Leigh W. *The Gay Decades: From Stonewall to the Present; The People and Events That Shaped Gay Lives.* New York: Plume [Penguin Books], 1992.
A date-by-date account of the struggle for American gay liberation, from Stonewall through 1990.

INTERNET RESOURCES

Due to the changeable nature of the Internet, sites appear and disappear very quickly. These resources offered useful information on Alan Turing at the time of publication. Internet addresses must be entered with capital and lowercase letters exactly as they appear.

http://www.yahoo.com
The *Yahoo* directory of the World Wide Web is an excellent place to find Internet sites on any topic.

http://www.wadham.ox.ac.uk/~ahodges/Turing.html
This page is maintained by Andrew Hodges, one of the foremost authorities on Alan Turing and author of *Alan Turing, the Enigma* (see Further Reading). It is a comprehensive electronic guide to Alan Turing's life and work. The page also contains links to many other sites on Alan Turing, as well as the history of computing in general.

http://www.cbi.umn.edu/welcome.htm
The Charles Babbage Institute (CBI) is a research center at the University of Minnesota dedicated to promoting the study and preservation of the history of information processing through historical research and archival activity.

INDEX